Advance praise for *Writing Alone, Writing Together*

"Writing groups . . . we writers have a love-hate relationship with them. Yet, there's no denying they are invaluable for building skills and confidence in our craft, and for enjoying camaraderie in an art that otherwise can be lonely indeed. When put together as Ms. Reeves describes here, you'll create a group that is supportive and nurturing. This is an important book for any new writer."

— Hal Zina Bennett, author of *Write from the Heart*

"*Writing Alone, Writing Together* is an impassioned call to write, one you will return to often for inspiration. Judy Reeves shows with engaging insight and clarity how writing with others can help you and your writing flourish. Judy genuinely loves writing and people who write (or want to!) and that creative energy makes every page of this book come alive."

— John Fox, author of *Poetic Medicine: The Healing Art of Poem-making* and *Finding What You Didn't Lose*

Praise for *A Writer's Book of Days*

"*A Writer's Book of Days* is the best sort of writer's book: You feel like writing as you read it! It is a spring-fed fountain of inspiration for the writers in us all. This book dances around the imagination and makes you take out your pens and journal to play."

— SARK, author/artist of *Succulent Wild Woman*

"The book is so jam-packed with inspiration, practical advice, and wise obser-vations and examples . . . that you feel yourself being eager to get at the writ-ing. . . . The method Judy Reeves uses is designed to make you dig deeper, free your creativity, and write, write, WRITE."

—*Writers' Journal*

Writing Alone,
Writing Together

Writing Alone, Writing Together

A Guide for Writers and Writing Groups

JUDY REEVES

NEW WORLD LIBRARY
NOVATO, CALIFORNIA

New World Library
14 Pamaron Way
Novato, California 94949

Front cover and text design by Mary Ann Casler
Typesetting by Tona Pearce Myers

Jan Phillips, "The Artist's Creed," from *Marry Your Muse*, published by Theosophical Publishing House. Copyright © 1997 by Jan Phillips. Reprinted by permission of the author.

Library of Congress Cataloging-in-Publication Data
Reeves, Judy
  Writing alone, writing together / Judy Reeves.
      p.   cm.
Includes bibliographical references.
  ISBN 978-1-57731-207-9 (pbk. : alk. paper)
  1. Authorship. 2. Authorship—Collaboration. I. Title.
  PN145 .R44 2002
  808'.02—dc21   2002006991

First Printing, October 2002
ISBN 978-1-57731-207-9

10 9 8 7 6 5 4 3 2

*For the generous writers who have included me in their writing communities
and for those who would be community makers*

CONTENTS

4   Read and Critique Groups   61

ACKNOWLEDGMENTS

Like writing itself, most of what I know about writing groups I have learned by participation and experience. From the youthful exuberance of my first group to the rich tapestry of my current involvement all these years later as both student and teacher, I am grateful for each of the groups I have been part of and for everything they have taught me about writing and life. There are far too many to list and I'm certain I wouldn't remember them all anyway, but I especially want to acknowledge the Brown Bag and Thursday Writers groups, the many and various marathon gatherings, and my Monday Night Read and Critique Group. The spirit and community of The Writing Center inspires me still.

I also want to thank the Journeymen Writing Group, where so much matters: Denise Nicholas; Rita Williams; Beverly Magid; Lisa Loop; Victoria Clayton-Alexander; Lavina Blossom, bright light in so many groups and gatherings; Amy Wallen, with whom I share the before and after and in-between; and my teacher and friend Janet Fitch.

The concepts for this book were formed amid the lively discussions and energetic exchanges that transpire during writing classes and in the sudden communities of writers conferences. However, it took the steady navigation and experienced hand of my editor, Georgia Hughes, for it to find solid ground. I am grateful for her trust and her equanimity.

My heartfelt thanks also go to:

Mary Ann Casler for another splendid cover and the fine crafting of interior design, and Tona Pearce Myers whose careful typesetting and attention to detail enhances the design.

Mike Ashby, whose observations and queries were as valuable as his copyediting. Maybe more so.

Dale Fetherling, who I count on for his expert wielding of editor's pen, which is always knowledgeable and sensitive.

Linda Corey and Lynne Friedmann for their thoughtful and generous comments on one of the many drafts of the manuscript.

Jan Rhodes for the play-by-play of the early structure of her writing group.

Diana Guerro for sharing her experience and perspective, and members of the Alliance of Writers for inviting me in.

The Compass Rose Travel Writers for use of their still-wet by laws.

Jan Phillips for her generosity and inspiration for community.

I'm indebted to my sister traveler and best writing friend, Dian Greenwood, and I'm thankful for the friendship, trust, and teaching I receive from Drusilla Campbell.

My life and work take shape with the love and support of my family and many generous, understanding, and good-humored friends. Always, I am grateful I get to share the journey with my friend Camille.

And for Roger, thank you for keeping the light burning.

INTRODUCTION

I think all artists, and especially poets, are forever in search of a community.
It's a solitary act, and you need a community of like-minded souls to survive
and to flourish. So the search of a community is really a lifetime engagement.
— Stanley Kunitz, U.S. Poet Laureate, 2000

Writing is a solitary act. We must do it alone. We must go into our own singular place of creation, where we sit long hours before our computer, or with pen in hand, notebook on table, and dip down into our own well. Even when we write together, we must go to the page alone. Even when we collaborate, each of us must pull needles from our own internal haystack.

Yet for all the ideas of writer as solitary, tortured soul alone in her cramped garret or shambled studio working into the night, in reality writers, like the rest of humanity, are basically communal creatures. We search out our own kind and build community as naturally as we breathe. It is within community we connect with others and, through our connecting, find home.

With few exceptions, we are not hermits or loners. We are social creatures. And, at the level of our creative efforts, we seek teachers, masters, and our fellows. Who else speaks our language, who else can understand, who else can help us over the high, rocky passes and through the valleys of our own shadows? It is too scary and hard to go it alone.

As long as we've been putting pen to page, we writers have come together for community. Percy Shelley, his wife, Mary Wollstonecraft Shelley, who wrote *Frankenstein,* and Lord Byron spent holidays together at Lake Geneva, writing; William Wordsworth, his sister, Dorothy, Samuel Coleridge, and the Hutchinson sisters, Sarah and Mary, called themselves "The Gang." There was the Lost Generation — Fitzgerald, Hemingway, Gertrude Stein, and other expatriates — in the fabled Paris of the twenties, and later in New York, the Algonquin Round Table with Dorothy Parker, Robert Benchley, George Kaufman, and others; later still, the Beats — Burroughs and Kerouac and Ginsberg. And today, on one coast or the other — the Nuyorican Poets Café or the Watts Writers Workshop — in the heartland (Heartland Writers Guild in Missouri), on the plains (Flathead River Writers of Montana), in the South (North Carolina Writers' Network), and globally on the Internet, writers seek out one another, connect, and create their art and create community.

I have been involved in writing groups in one way or another since I was eleven years old, when my sister, my best friend, Betty Barnes, and I agreed to write stories together and to read them to each other. My first story was titled "Three Buckets of Blood," a tale in which vampires take over the chicken coop in our backyard. By then, I had been a writer for nearly three years, having named myself one in third grade. My work as a solitary writer and as a member of any number of writing groups continues to this day, nearly half a century later.

Though ultimately it is the page that teaches us to write, in my years of experience as a writing teacher and as a participant of many, many writing groups, I've come to believe that it is working within the community of other writers that we learn the craft, the discipline, and the process of our art. This is where we become Writers.

Many individual writers — especially beginning or beginning-again writers — try to go it alone. They struggle to find the time to write, they set goals and make resolutions that fall by the way of whatever seems more pressing. Or, they begin pieces that never get completed, either because they get stuck and don't know what to do next, or because the

"We are not a society of rugged individualists who wish to go it alone, but a communal people who want to band together in mutual support."

— Robert Wuthnow

voice of the inner critic tells them the work is no good. In the absence of any encouragement, self-doubt wrestles desire to the ground. Into the drawer these pieces go. Or into the trash bin. And the would-be writer is left with a sense of utter failure at what she longs most to do.

Many years passed between my first exciting plunge into the deep and often murky waters of writing and my current immersion as a committed writer and member of a lively writing community. I was one of those "beginning-again" writers, hanging around the edges of the writing pond, barely daring to stick a toe in, yet longing to dive in headfirst. Though I'd participated in many groups, it wasn't until I met and partnered up with my best writing friend, Dian, that I finally dared to take the leap. We've been writing together for more than a decade. Regularly. Consistently. And getting better as a result.

I've seen this happen again and again. Writers who could never get started and keep going on their own take wing and soar with the support and nurturance of a writing partner or group.

At the beginning of my writing classes, I always ask my students why they joined the group. They respond:

"I only write when I have a deadline and a place to show up."
"If I'm in a group, I know I will produce."
"I need the input of other writers."
"I need the group for the discipline of it."

The idea of having a time and place to be with a completed assignment is what motivates many, many writers to keep at it. And not just beginners.

Most writers I know are ongoing, steady participants in some kind of a writing community — whether it's just one other person or a structured group of four to twenty writers or an informal gathering of friends and colleagues. Review the acknowledgments section of any number of books and you'll often see thanks expressed for the author's writing friends and colleagues.

Writers working with other writers is an integral and necessary part

"You write and while you write you are ashamed for everyone must think you are a crazy one and yet you write and you know you will be laughed at or pitied by everyone and you are not very certain and you go on writing. Then someone says 'yes' to it and never again can you have completely such a feeling of being afraid and ashamed that you had when you were writing and not any one had said 'yes' about the thing."

— Gertrude Stein

of the writing process. So much of what we do we must do alone. Thus finding our own kind to share the joy and the pain, the exhilaration and the drudgery is sometimes a necessary survival mechanism. A writing community that supports and nurtures us and cheers us on is what makes the solitary work bearable. It is the work we do "alone, together."[1]

Writing groups are where we learn our craft, too. Read and critique groups, writing practice groups, workshop groups — all these offer feedback, tips and ideas, how-tos, and suggestions. Often it is only after we begin to work with a group that we are able to find our writing voice and to create and evaluate our work.

In writing groups, we bear witness to each other's efforts, we learn from one another, and spark each other's creativity. We share camaraderie and create community. It is in writing groups that we find our tribe.

Yet, for all the books about writing and for all the urging of writers to get into a group, guidelines for forming and running such groups are few — usually a chapter at the back of a book about the craft. Many writers who would love to be a part of a lively and supportive writing community don't know where to find one, how to start one, or what to do once they're in one.

It's my hope that this book can answer some questions, provide information, offer up a few ideas for forming and sustaining writing groups, and serve as a companion along the way for those who are seeking and creating their own writing community.

The book is the result of my experience in writing groups, first as a writer and then as a teacher. What I know is this: Like the writing itself, each writing group takes on a life and energy of its own.

Though I have attempted to describe and present different types of groups in an organization that found its way out of scores of examples and thick files of notes and references, like the writing itself, there will always be exceptions and nuances and quirks and one-offs that defy

"...one of the ways we know we are writers is when writers tell us so, pointing out a way through the dark wood."

— Nicholas Delbanco

---

1. The term "alone/together" comes from concepts presented in *At a Journal Workshop* by Ira Progoff (New York: Tarcher, 1992).

labeling and fly in the face of organization. Good. We need a measure of unpredictability — in our lives and our art. So as you read through the descriptions of different types of writing groups, know that the guidelines presented are not rigid, but rather strands of ideas meant to be woven together in patterns that will be unique to each weaver.

The chapters that follow address the writer who works alone, as all of us must. And, for some, working alone is as good as it gets. But this book is written primarily for the writer who wants to be in community with other writers in some type of writing group, and for writing groups that may be looking for structure or guidelines as they come together, or for ideas and suggestions to expand beyond their original form. In addition to information about writing groups in general, three types of writing groups are presented: the read and critique group, the writing practice group, and the writing workshop group.

A read and critique group is one in which participants critique material written outside the group. Usually these groups include a steady and fixed membership of peers, all working at about the same level.

In writing practice groups, things are a bit more spontaneous. During the meetings, a writing prompt is given and participants go to it without any further direction, spontaneously getting on the page whatever comes. There is no critique or feedback after the writing is completed, but the work is almost always read aloud.

In a writing workshop group, participants create new material based on an aspect of the craft, or they work on particular projects, usually with specific guidelines or instruction. Four types of workshop groups are included: elements of the craft, exploring your voice, project groups, and common grounds groups.

Each of the writing groups may borrow techniques from the others, especially workshop groups which may use the principles of writing practice in the creation of new material, and when writers have had a chance to edit and rewrite their material, read and critique might be a part of the session. And, as I say, the threads are loose. You and your group may create a macramé of your own unique and imaginative design

Keys to Marginalia

♀ Exploration invites you to go within through the intuitive use of freewriting, to discover thoughts and feelings you may not be aware of on a conscious level.

•➔ Exercise is a suggested writing assignment designed to help you clarify, define, discover, or name elements that are important to you.

✓ Checklists are a quick way to make lists and present information.

▱ Quotes from other writers or taken from within the text.

† Typecasting writers gives broad generalizations of behavior and characteristics of some types of writers I've observed in groups.

†† Information and material for writing groups.

✐ Writing practice prompts to jumpstart any practice session.

whose knots hold you together in a community of lively camaraderie and solid support. I hope you'll share your good ideas with me.

Scattered along the margins throughout the book are checklists and inventories that provide quick overviews, as well as ideas, tips, how-tos, guidelines, and a few words of advice and inspiration. You'll also find suggestions for exercises and explorations that invite you to plumb your experiences and beliefs about writing and writing groups.

The final chapter — Beyond Groups — takes the writer and the group into the larger community of conferences, retreats, writers colonies, and professional organizations. This chapter also suggests ways writers can give back to the community in which they live, offering gifts both literary and personal. Through sharing our art we make the world a better place, and writers remind the rest of the community that by giving rise to our voices and telling our stories we stay connected as human beings.

1 WRITING ALONE

A Writer Is Someone Who Writes

Gertrude Stein wrote, "To write is to write is to write is to write is to write is to write is to write." Who can say what she meant (she also wrote, "Rose is a rose is a rose is a rose"), except perhaps exactly what she wrote: that writing is all and everything of it, the beginning and the end. That to write is to write. We just do it. How to get started writing? Write. How to keep going? Write.

Sadly, for many of us it just isn't that simple. We have trouble getting started, we have trouble keeping the pace and, too often, we simply give up or our enthusiasm and determination trickle away, like a stream petering out.

But because writing is in our hearts and souls and DNA, after a few weeks or months or even years, we're back at it again. More determined than ever that, this time, we'll stay with it.

Maybe we do and maybe we don't. In my experience as a teacher, more often than not people don't stay with it. For some, the cycle repeats and repeats. Because we can't keep the thing going, we begin to judge ourselves failures at writing, our self-esteem goes the way of our tossed out pages, and after a while, it becomes more and more difficult to begin again.

This is heartbreaking. Because we are writers and when we aren't being fully and wholly ourselves — when a piece of ourselves is missing — we can never feel at home in the world or at peace within ourselves.

1

Writing is who we are. Not all of who we are, but enough of who we are that when we're not writing, we're not whole.

Claim Yourself As Writer

Until you name yourself Writer, you will never be a writer who writes (and keeps writing).

Most writers I know, especially those who have not published, say, "I want to be a writer." Or "I'm a [fill in the blank] and I like to write." Or "I've always dreamed of being a writer." But they don't actually call themselves a writer. Think of all the other names you give yourself: man/woman, mother/father, wife/husband, friend, teacher, technician, masseuse, lawyer, gardener, chef. We take each of these names as a way of identifying ourselves, both to others and to ourselves. We are what we say we are. In some cultures, new names are assumed when character-evolving events take place. These names indicate the person has been transformed.

If you announce you *are* a writer, rather than simply mouthing that you want to be or you'd like to be, you may be transformed. Try it. Right now. Speak your name out loud followed by, "I'm a writer." Let yourself experience the sensations you feel when you sound out the words.

"But I haven't been published yet," you might say, as if this were the thing that would give you the right to call yourself writer. After all, when you tell people you're a writer, don't they always ask, "Oh, and what have you published?"

Listen to this: Being published doesn't have anything to do with being a writer! It has to do with earning money as a writer. Maybe. Getting some kind of validation and recognition, perhaps notoriety and fame. Though truth be told, the majority of published writers don't earn all that much money or notoriety or fame. We might say, to be published is to be published is to be published. To be sure, getting published is the aim of many of us. After all, we write to communicate, and having an audience is the flip side of the communication coin. But it is not the reason we write. We write because it is what we must do. Anne Sexton said, "When I am writing I am doing the thing I was meant to do."

Success for a writer doesn't necessarily mean being published (but it can), or even making a living as a writer. Each of us must determine our own version of success. For some it's writing every day, for others it's completing a particular project. Do a five-minute freewriting that begins, "When I'm a successful writer I..."

Besides, once we are published, this doesn't mean we will stop writing. We will continue to write. This is what writers do. I have this vision of me at my writing table, a fat roll of butcher's paper at one end and a take-up reel with a crank at the other end. The paper just keeps passing beneath my pen and I just keep writing. As the old joke goes, "Old writers never die, they just keep revising the ending."

How do you claim yourself as writer?

First, say it. "I'm a writer." Say it out loud. Say it to yourself in the mirror. Say it to your friends and family. Say it to the next person you meet at a party who asks, "What do you do?" Say it to a stranger in line at the grocery store. Say it to your mother. Mostly, say it to yourself. "I'm a writer."

- Make a place for your writing, a sacred place where you go with joy as your companion, not dread or guilt or "shoulds" riding your shoulders like weights of sand. If you don't already have a room or specific place, make one. Take up a whole room or a section of a room. Before she created her own studio, my friend Wendy used a screen to separate her writing place from the rest of the living room. If the only space you can free up for your writing is part of a table, sometimes, when you're not eating on it, then make it a special place. When you go there for your writing, bring along a candle or lamp or some flowers, anything that transforms the space from the quotidian to the unique. Make it important and make it yours however you can. Claim the space.

- Get the tools you need. Honor your writing with the kind of paper or notebook you like; buy your favorite pens by the box or spend a bundle on that Waterman or Mont Blanc you've always wanted. Have a computer that belongs to you — not one you have to share — and a good printer. It's amazing what just printing out your writing using a laser jet printer will do to make it look — and you

Create a biography of yourself as writer. Begin with your earliest memory of "being a writer," and follow the path of your writing journey up to the present day. Include stops and starts along the way, high points and lows, celebrations and doubts. List groups you belonged to and projects you started (and completed, or not). Take your time and let memories surface. After you've completed your history, reread what you've written to discover patterns or recurring cycles.

It may not be an entire "room of our own," but each of us needs to have our own writing space. Take five minutes for a freewriting that begins, "My ideal writing space is . . ." After you've completed this exploration, do another freewriting that describes your current writing space. If the two don't match up (and they probably won't), give some thought to ways you can transfer some of your "ideals" into your present-day situation.

feel — professional. Get a good dictionary, thesaurus, and stylebook. Find books on the craft and subscribe to writing journals.

- Hang out with other writers. Go to readings and book signings, open mikes. Communicate with other writers. Drop a note to someone whose book you admire and tell them (not in a gushy, fan magazine kind of way, but as one writer to another). Sign up for workshops and conferences. Get in a group.

- Read as a writer. Learn from the best. Study your favorite authors, and copy passages into your notebook to get the feel of their rhythm and style. Deconstruct their sentences, paragraphs, scenes, and chapters to discover their techniques and their secrets. Read the work aloud and discuss the books with your writer friends. Next to the act of writing itself, reading good writing will be your best teacher.

Make Time to Write

The second thing you must do to be a writer who writes is make the time to write. This is where many would-be writers fall short. Unless you make the time to write, you'll never write. Extra time won't just show up, and if you promise to do your writing "as soon as . . ." you'll never get to it. Take it from one who knows. For the better part of twenty-five years, I was a writer who would write "as soon as . . ."; I had more stops and starts in my writing career than a local train. It wasn't until I actually set aside writing time on a regular basis that I became a writer who writes.

Make an appointment with your writing self, write it down in your calendar: 2:00 P.M. Monday: Write; 3:30 P.M. Tuesday: Write; 9:15 A.M. Wednesday: Write; and so forth.

Find a time that fits you. Don't set aside two hours if you can only do thirty minutes. Don't set your alarm for 5:30 in the morning if you always resist getting up and hate the mornings. You may come to resent your writing as much as you resent the alarm clock. By the same token, don't say you'll do it at night after everything else is done if, by 8:30, you're supine on the couch and can't keep your eyes open. Find a time that works for you. Take half your lunch hour. Do it right after work. Get up half an hour earlier. If you have the flexibility to make your own schedule, set aside time during the workday.

In my classes I listen to the complaints of students who say they just don't have time to write, then I ask for a show of hands of those who watch television on a regular basis or those who surf the Web. When the rows of hands waving in the air look like an Iowa cornfield in August, I ask again, "Who can't find the time to write?" Sheepish grins and embarrassed giggles. Write instead of watching TV, instead of surfing the Web, instead of spending an hour or more reading the newspaper, instead of going out with friends. You have to give up something. Even if it's only leisure time in front of the tube.

Note: don't give up taking walks or witnessing sunsets.

You may have always heard that if you want to be a writer, you have to write every day. This is not an absolute rule. Few rules are. To be successful (i.e., a writer who writes), you do have to write several times a week — at least four or five sessions, and every day is best. Pulitzer Prize-winning author Michael Chabon swears by his 10 P.M. to 4 A.M. Sunday-Thursday routine. Part of it is the daily habit of it and part of it is the continuity. The writing will come easier with regular practice, too. You get better at something you do often. Mick Jagger said, "You have to sing every day so you can build up to being, you know, Amazingly Brilliant."

In a *New Yorker* (January 28, 2002) article titled "The Learning Curve — How Do You Become a Good Surgeon? Practice," Atul Gawande related the importance of practice. In writing about elite performers, he said, "[T]he most important talent may be the talent for practice itself." He referred to K. Anders Ericsson, a psychologist, who noted that "the most important role that innate factors play may be in a person's *willingness* to engage in sustained training."

Like exercise or losing weight or taking a class, sometimes it's a whole lot easier to do it with a supportive companion. Make a date with

Keep a writing calendar. For a month, note the times you wrote and the times you planned to write and didn't (and what interfered with your plans.) This exercise is especially helpful for those who have difficulty sustaining a writing practice, or keeping writing dates with themselves. If writing down the times you plan to write helps you keep to your practice, keep doing it!

a friend for writing. If you can't get together in person, make a phone call or e-mail one another to say, "I wrote today" or "I'm going to write at 6:30 this evening," or "How'd the writing go today?"

Waiting for inspiration to descend before you write is like waiting for Godot. Interminable. It's been said that if you show up at your page at the agreed upon time, inspiration will know where to find you. Someone else said, "Writing is 20 percent inspiration and 80 percent perspiration." Besides, if writing is your daily practice, you won't need inspiration to get to it. Imagine waiting for inspiration to rest her shining arms around you before you take the dog for a walk or drive to work.

Write

Finally, the third leg in the triangle of being a writer who writes is, of course, doing the thing. Talking about writing isn't writing. Thinking about writing isn't writing. Dreaming or fantasizing isn't writing. Neither are outlining, researching, or making notes. All these may be a part of the whole milieu of the writing life and necessary to getting a project completed, but only writing is writing.

"You can't sit around thinking," said fiction writer David Long. "You must sit around writing."

So every day, at the appointed time (or at some spontaneous gift of time), you sit at your desk (or your table in the café or on the grass in the park), you open your notebook or you boot up your computer, and you write.

Do this every day and I will guarantee you, you will fill notebook after notebook, you will begin and complete stories, essays, narrative nonfiction — whatever you want to write. You will have bits and pieces and wild, imaginative ramblings. You will be a Writer Who Writes.

The Candle, the Prayer, the Morning Light: Rites and Rituals, Methods and Disciplines of the Writer

The small crystal pyramid on the windowsill catches morning light that laces through thick leaves of the avocado tree in the backyard. On the

---

⚲ Three Easy Steps to Becoming a Writer Who Writes

1. Claim yourself as writer
2. Make time to write
3. Write

table, a book of meditations; pressed to the window ledge, a prayer written on a yellow sticky note. There is a candle, a blue one for serenity and peace. There is coffee in a black ceramic mug and three thick-nibbed pens. She has already worked through her morning exercises and stretched and downed a bottle of water. The neighbor's dog has already come for his morning treat, his tail thumping against the wooden boards of the porch. Now, it is time to write.

She will light the candle. She will say the prayer. She will read the meditation, and then she will open her notebook and begin. It is her morning ritual.

One or two days in the week, she gathers all her notebooks and sits before her computer and enters page after page of the raw, rough writing she's scratched out. Copying word for messy word, the scrawled convolutions and mixed metaphors and even the occasional fine image or phrase. She inputs all the intentions and ideas and half-wrought imagery. Mostly she does this without judgment. That comes later.

When all the pages are transferred from notebook birthing place to computer cradle, she will save them in files, print them out, take them to her kitchen table or spread them out on the couch beneath the brass lamp, or pack them up and take them to a café, where she'll order an Americano (single, with room for cream), and read what's there. She'll scrawl notes to herself and change words or phrases, stretch long lines between this paragraph and that, altering the order. In go the asterisks with accompanying notes of what to add or take away, doodles of little doors that mean "enter here, go deeper," references to what rouses her curiosity. And for days, back and forth she'll travel between computer and notebook, covering page after page with her blue-tinged notes until she can't read the paper and must start anew. Until finally, she's nearly satisfied with the draft of a scene or a story or a narrative that she'll take to her group for read and critique.

Then it's back to the beginning. The candle. The prayer. The morning sun filtering through the thick green leaves of the avocado tree.

Write about your rituals and routines. Include where you write and when, what you do before and after. List what mementos or keepsakes you have in your writing space and what they mean to you. Include how you dress, what tools you use, and any other particulars that have to do with your writing practice.

This is one person's practice. Ask any writer and you'll get the same kind of detailed answer. We all have our ceremonies and rituals that don't so much accompany our writing as form part and parcel of the whole thing.

Schiller sniffed his rotten fruit, Dumas *père* ate his morning apple beneath the Arc de Triomphe. Stephen King has "my glass of water, my vitamin pill, my music, my same seat, and the papers all arranged in the same places." Willa Cather read the Bible; Stendhal read the French civil code. We have our coffee or tea or stiff bourbon at 5:00 P.M.; we munch on nuts or raisins or M&Ms or red licorice or raw carrots. We write our ten pages before noon or we walk our twenty blocks before we begin. Music or silence, before the sun rises or after it sets, writing by hand or strictly by computer. These are the things we do.

If you will take the time to write down all the different rites and observances you go through to do your writing, you may surprise yourself. Some practices you didn't even know you performed may be an important part of the way you make your art. "Without even knowing it, I had developed a 'practice,'" wrote Gail Sher in *One Continuous Mistake: Four Noble Truths for Writers*. "Every day, no matter what, I wrote one haiku. In my mind I became the person who writes 'a haiku a day.' That was the beginning of knowing who I was."

Your patterns have significance. And, unless you examine them, you may never know what lies beneath the need to have fresh flowers on your desk each Thursday or to surround yourself with objects of natural beauty such as shells and stones and feathers and twigs. Our rituals carry as much information about us as our DNA, though they may be more difficult to interpret.

Like any rituals, those we practice as we do our writing will take on more meaning if we do them with mindfulness and intention. When we realize what matters to us and incorporate this knowledge into our writing, we will receive more from our work. By being present and paying attention, our work becomes ritual, and the daily practice of it deepens our connection with ourselves and enriches and nourishes us.

"The creation of ritual is a universal human impulse. We all do and say things without perceptible practical reasons, other than to reassure ourselves with empowering or repetitive thoughts and behaviors."

— Barbara Walker

The Magic Key: Routines and Eccentricities

Each of us must find our own style of writing and develop routines that support it. Just like being most at ease when we dress in a manner that's comfortable to us, when we follow our own style of writing rather than what someone else dictates, we become less self-conscious, we feel more authentic. Defenses are dropped. Now we can get to the real stuff.

Like our writer whose practices began this section, you may be a by-hand-only notebook writer, while someone else can work only on his laptop. Even at the beach or schlepped from car to café to nightstand. He believes that's why God invented the battery pack. Writing by the dawn's early light or beneath the waxing moon. Writing naked or dressing up in the costumes of our characters. Wearing a patchy old "lucky" sweater or a Cincinnati Reds baseball cap. Standing up, sitting down, or lying in bed amid a mound of pillows. No matter what someone else does, we must find our own way.

At readings or seminars, when time comes for Q&A, someone will invariably ask the famous writer, "How do you write?" or "What is your writing routine?" As if, because she's successful and famous, this writer will have the magic key that will open the doors to the Sacred Palace of Mystical Writers where the secrets of success are kept, and we will all (at least those of us who are lucky enough to be present), finally, be able to enter.

But what the famous writer says is generally so mundane we think we might have misunderstood. "I get up in the morning and begin writing where I left off the day before." "I read some poetry then I go to my desk and I begin to write." "I answer my mail, make a few phone calls, then I sit down and write."

Almost always, the famous writer concludes with "and then I begin to write." This, then, is the magic key. Whatever you do before or after, whatever styles and routines and individual eccentricities you develop "and then I begin to write" must be part of your routine. Regular, on-going, continuous.

"People are made differently, and receive or coerce their ideas in unpredictable rhythms. But the fact is that most productive writers show up for work as dutifully and with as little fanfare as any civil servant."

— Rosellen Brown

Disciples of Writing

Somewhere along the way, the word *discipline* came to mean something harsh or cruel. A sort of *hut-two-three-four* Marine Corps mentality at the least and a switch to the bare bottom at the worst. In reality, it's nothing like that at all. The word *discipline* comes from the Latin for teaching, learning. A disciple is a pupil or a student.

We are all disciples of our writing. And as such, we must be disciplined. We must exercise the kind of self-control that gets us to our writing place every day, that turns down invitations and turns off the television. Nobody will do these things for us. There is not a mommy who will take away our dessert, no teacher to give us an F, no drill sergeant to put us on report. Self-discipline is all we have.

And in the end it serves us well. How else will we complete a three-hundred-page novel or a three-thousand-word essay or a three-line haiku without the kind of stick-to-itiveness that borders the paths of all works, great and small? No matter how much we love writing, it is still the discipline that keeps us true to our love.

Such structure may be hard to come by, especially for the beginning writer who has yet to learn that there will always be hard places, slippery places, stuck places, scary places. Places where it might seem easier just to fold the tent and steal into the night and who's to know. This writer, or the beginning-again writer, who is perhaps more the one who needs to pay attention to discipline, can remind himself that, no matter what, just keep working. Most likely you will get to the other side if you keep after it, but for certain, if you give up, the other side becomes as elusive as any magic key or sacred palace.

Sometimes, for the beginning writer or the beginning-again writer who's in a wiggly place, it can help to call a friend, enroll in a class, sign up for a workshop, or commit to a group. We may need to borrow some discipline from time to time, and there's nothing wrong with that. Every pantry runs out of sugar on occasion. Even writers who've been at it awhile may find discipline a hard commodity to come by. Remember the story of Eugène Ionesco, who had his wife lock him in the cellar, or the rumor of the writer who supposedly

"Be regular and ordinary in your habits, like a petit bourgeois, so you may be violent and original in your work."

— Gustave Flaubert

tied the silken belt of his robe to the arms of his chair to keep him-self at work.

Routines and rituals, discipline and structure: it is within this order that the wild, free creative mind is set loose to roam.

Surrender to the Page

Remember all the times you took your notebook to the café, ordered your latte, found a quiet table by the window or in the corner — wher-ever you were least likely to be distracted — and just wrote? You didn't have any intentions for the writing, or any expectations. You just wrote.

Or the times beneath the sycamore tree in the park, or in the shade beside the river, or in your car parked at the viewpoint above the ocean as gulls swooped outside your open window? In your bed at night with pil-lows piled high behind you and a mug of chamomile tea within sipping range, notebook propped on jammied knee? Writing about thunderstorms in August when lightning flings a sideways strike across the sky or the smell of lavender in your grandmother's bedroom, the dark furniture and papered walls? The taste of strawberries fresh picked from the garden?

All those times just you and your notebook, writing, writing, writ-ing. When you lost track of time and place and even yourself, and rode the sweet edge of imagination, your pen as vessel and your note-book, the deep reaches of inner or outer space you explored.

This is writing practice. The occasion in which you are able to move out of your self-consciousness and surrender to the page. You become the writing. This state of total engrossment is what psychologist Mihaly Csikszentmihalyi calls "flow." You are absolutely in the moment, doing what you are doing, unconscious of time or place or the space around you. "If you are a writer, writing and being are the same," wrote Gail Sher.

When you write in this manner, you are practicing your craft, you're honoring your practice of writing and yourself as writer.

Writing practice is what writers do naturally. Like imagining and wondering and daydreaming. It's only when we begin to have expecta-tions of ourselves or our writing that we resist what is so normal to us.

"I consider the gift of being absorbed into my work the greatest pleasure and the noblest privilege of my life."

— Ursula K. Le Guin

Then writing becomes a series of "shoulds" (I should finish that story, I should write more often, I should write something important, I should get this stuff together and try to publish it). For us, writing practice is like breathing; we need never remind ourselves we *should*.

Within the daily ritual of writing practice, the stories that want to be written find their way from our deepest self and onto our pages. We may not even know what these stories are. One of the most common remarks heard in writing practice groups is, "I don't know where that came from." This, after a writer reads from her notebook what she has written and is utterly amazed at what she finds on her page. (The other common remark is, "I can't read my own handwriting," which comes, too, after a writer has lost himself to the moment and handwriting, spelling, grammar, and other elements of style are dust in the wind of this reckoning with truth.)

When we are called to writing, in contrast to those who find their voice through music or by flinging paint onto canvas or hunched over the potter's wheel or any other creative expressions of our experience, we don't always know what we want to write about. We may think we know. Ideas come to us brilliant as fireworks or slip into our dreams silken as moths' wings, but even as we try to put these ideas into words, what we really want to write about appears on the page as if by a magic solution applied to disappearing ink. Words and images form, seemingly out of nowhere, and rush onto the page in a surge of energy as unstoppable as a birth.

"Where did that come from?"

You can trust what appears in your notebook during writing practice. This is where your authentic voice explores its range. The noise you make on the page — ungainly and messy as it may be — is your own true voice. Consider practice to be voice lessons.

Of course, there is a time when the writer must move back from the practice and step into the second role of editor, paging through the material to discover what stories lie within all these rambling pages. Just as there is a time to let loose and let fly, there comes a time to sort through the chaos of the practice notebook to find the spine of the

Every writer has his or her own reasons and motives for putting words on paper, but not all of us know what they are. For this exploration, let your inner writer have a say. Don't think of reasons why you write, just begin a ten-minute freewriting with, "I write because . . ." and remember to trust your pen and the process.

creature that we have formed. These bones we will lift as carefully as an archaeologist and place into the transformative technology of our computers, where we will rearrange and chip away and add to and polish up as best we can into the shape that the spine suggests. But this is not the same function as practice. At the computer, we use both sides of the brain. As our own editors we analyze and judge and compare and measure and qualify. But at the time of practice, we abandon all that, take off the protective eyeshade of the editor, and get ourselves as much out of the way as possible.

Why Practice?

"But does all this practice ever really produce anything?" you may ask. My students ask this question all the time. At least those who are new to the practice of practice. "I mean what's the point?" they say. "I fill my notebook and then start another and *what?*"

After nearly a decade of regular writing practice, done both alone and with groups, here's what I know:

Notebooks will be filled. Page after page of your original writing. Not all of it good. But not all of it bad, either. And some of it will be absolutely gorgeous. For some writers, this is enough. Making daily contact with their writing self is a way of touching home. It is an affirmation of their deepest longing. For them, the process is what matters most.

Others discover what they want to write about. Through practice sessions where no directive is given except *Write,* they find their voice and the genre in which it hits the truest notes. Some, who thought they wanted to write memoirs, might be surprised to hear the chatter of fictional characters joining in the re-created dialogue of nearest and dearest. ("Where did that come from?") I know a poet who began writing personal narrative essays during practice times and a fiction writer who turned to screenplays. A woman who intended to write screenplays found herself reliving her Berkshires childhood, creating full and rounded sketches of aunts and cousins and detailed stories of her mother.

Many fiction writers use practice sessions to explore scenes and characters. The better part of my novel found its way out of writing

In your notebook begin a paragraph with, "I want to write about . . ." and freewrite a few sentences without thinking about what you want to write. After you've written three or four sentences that include some specific details, drop down a line and begin a new paragraph with the same prompt: "I want to write about . . ." Again, freewrite without thinking, just let the images and words pour from pen to page, bypassing the conscious brain. If you fill one page in your notebook, you should have four or five subjects.

practice beginnings. Instead of writing from my own point of view, I turn the pages over to Lily or Louise or Anna. And I'm not the only one who writes fiction this way. Amy and Joe and Greg and Steve and Wendy and David and Lavina and Dian are just a few of the fiction writers I know who use practice sessions to create the first raw drafts of their stories. Something about the freedom and no-holds-barred atmosphere of a practice session encourages the authentic expression these writers crave. Like dancing without a partner. It's not about following or leading, you just give yourself over to the music.

Then there is the freedom to take risks. You can try anything. What the heck, this is just practice. You can always tear out the page. Nobody has to actually see those fumbling attempts at haiku. Or the outrageous made-up monologue of your aunt who used to be a go-go dancer, big hair, white boots, fluorescent body paint and all. You can write the things that scare you most even as you cross out every other word and your handwriting gets more pinched and crabbed with every line and you can hardly breathe. Still, you keep going because it is, after all, only practice.

Practice is trying out ideas and auditioning words and writing nonsense and secrets and lies. It is the equivalent of an artist's sketchbook for writers. It is liberating and joyful and playful and exciting and surprising and spontaneous and fulfilling. It is a place for grieving and healing and working through and remembering and recovering. It is expansive.

Give Us This Day

Writing practice is best done daily. It is the both the habit of showing up each day and the cumulative effect of each day's work that will finally shape you. Think of the river ever running its wet tongue over rocky walls, or the wind ceaselessly breathing against ragged cliff stone.

Writing practice is best done at a certain time every day. Like arising, brushing your teeth, making the coffee, letting out the dog — any of the daily routines that you perform without thinking — daily writing practice becomes habit. You don't have to plan to set aside the time

"…the act of writing itself, that mysterious, dangerous, intoxicating, absorbing nourishing magical trick that act of creation generates its own light."

— Janette Turner Hospital

or mark these activities down on your appointment calendar, you simply do them. (Until you find the best time for your work and before your daily practice becomes routine, putting it on your calendar is a good way to remind yourself of your commitment.)

Also, when you practice at the same time every day, you send a message to your creative self. Like the body preparing to receive massage when you hoist yourself onto the massage table, your creative self will switch into ready mode when the time comes for writing. Writing practice is best done in a specific place every day. The monks of old called their writing places "scriptoria." These were holy places and the work performed there was considered sacred. So it is with writing practice. You honor your writing and your writing self when you create a special place for your work. Bring to it all that supports and enhances your writing. Keep it clean and free from clutter. You know the old saying that a cluttered desk is the sign of a cluttered mind. With all that mess, how can thoughts emerge without their edges catching on whatever is left lying around? Gather round you items that bring you pleasure and evoke creativity. Surround yourself with beauty, for "beauty is to enthuse us for work," wrote Polish poet Cyprian Norwid, "and work is to raise it up." Collect and display those things that are meaningful to you. Call this place sacred and claim it as your own holy place. Light a candle before you begin. Offer up a prayer.

This is not to say you must practice only at this time and in this place. Spontaneity adds to writing as a measure of herbs enhances a stew. Take your notebook with you anywhere and everywhere. Plan writing practice field trips — the Beyond Borders exhibit at the museum of photography (write about the photographs and your response to them), the airport, where you go not to board a plane but people-watch and make notes. Take a trip to Thursday's farmers market. Sample and taste and write it down. Surprise the muse by showing up where she least expects you. She adores spontaneity.

Practice is not just to get better at something. Practice is how you become what you want to be. For most practitioners I know, Writer is what they want to be. To my mind, the only way to be a writer is to write.

❧

Plan writing field trips. Set aside a few hours to take your notebook or your laptop "on location." Cafés, sure, but be a bit more adventurous. Points of arrival and departure (the bus station has a completely different ambiance than the airport). Sit in on proceedings in a court of law, hang out at a realtor's open house, make notes from the balcony of a theater during different kinds of performances, people watch at a street fair or auction or ball game. You get the idea. Go alone or with a writing chum.

✓ Keep the Fire Burning

As a checklist, ask yourself the following questions, which are, in themselves, building blocks for a sustainable process. How you answer them will tell you where you might need to make changes or focus your attention. Answer each question with true/false, yes/no, or always/sometimes/never, whichever works for you. And if you go beyond one-word answers and use your notebook to write a few sentences in response to the questions, you might find yourself in a heart-to-heart dialogue with your writer-self.

1. I identify myself as writer. When someone asks me what I do, I answer, "I'm a writer." Or at least I always include it. "I earn my living as a teacher, and I'm a writer." Or, "I'm a writer and my day job is biomedical research."

2. I give myself affirmations, claiming myself as writer: notes in my notebook or journal, stuck on my bulletin board or computer, on the bathroom mirror; or by saying them out loud to myself. "I am a writer writing." "I honor myself when I write." "I am most authentic when I write." (These may sound silly, but writing affirmations really works. Take it from someone who's done it.)

3. I have a special writing space. Even if I actually write all over town — in cafés, in my car, at the beach, at the Laundromat — I maintain a sacred space for my writing.

4. I have the tools and materials and support I need. Computer, printer, notebooks, reference books, pens. I buy or check out from the library books or tapes about writing and subscribe to literary journals and writing publications.

5. I have writing friends with whom I write or talk about writing or do writing activities.

6. I do writerly things: I'm a member of a writing group, I go to readings. I read interviews with writers and listen to

what they have to say about the art and craft and life of being a writer.

7. I write to writers whose work has influenced me, and thank them. These aren't "fan" letters, but I claim myself as writer and tell them what their work means to me — writer to writer.

8. I make time for my writing on a regular basis.

9. When I can't keep my writing date, I acknowledge why (in other words, I don't just blow it off), and reschedule.

10. When I see that I consistently break my appointments, I review what might be going on, and make changes where necessary.
    - I've chosen a time that really doesn't work for me.
    - It's an especially busy time in my life (moving, house-guests, something unexpected, other deadlines).
    - I've set my goals too high (no way can I write two hours a day! What was I thinking?).
    - Other_____(fill in the blank).

11. I put my writing time way up there on my priorities list. Not some vague "as soon as" or "when I can" or "if I have time today."

12. I set aside enough time to build consistency — not just once a week, or when I have a few days free, but if not daily, at least several times a week, more days writing than not.

13. I create special times for writing — a long weekend or a retreat (with other writers or by myself) or to participate in a conference or a seminar where I'll actually write.

14. I write. When I go to my writing space, when I set aside the time, when I meet my friends, I don't just think about writing or talk about writing. I write.

15. When I'm stuck, I find out what's holding me back. When I procrastinate, I acknowledge that's what I'm doing. When I'm afraid, I face my fear and write through it. And when all is said and done, I write.

② WRITING TOGETHER

Kindred Spirits Speaking a Common Language

One bright winter Tuesday at our regular Brown Bag meeting, a novelist I hadn't seen in years dropped in. What a surprise! The last I'd heard of her, literally, was on the radio voicing another of her charming and funny personal essays that were regular installments on NPR. But here she was, bound galley of her fifth novel under her arm, ready to open her notebook and write with the rest of us.

I guess I assumed that any writer with that much experience and success behind her wouldn't need a gathering such as ours. But she told me how she longed to be with other writers. It helped her get grounded again, she said, and to get perspective on a broader world. "I need to come out at least once a day to see if anyone else is out there." She laughed as if she felt a little embarrassed admitting it.

Except for a very few of us — religious recluses and true hermits — if we're alone with ourselves for too long, our focus gets too narrow; our view too introspective. We sense a need within, a yearning for connection with others. This is the reason, I think, for the constant flow of e-mail messages and phone calls I receive from writers of all sorts looking for a group to join.

"Where can I find a read and critique group?" "How can I get in a beginners' writing group?" "Do you know any groups that are accepting new members?"

In writing groups, we come together for community and connection. We may believe it has everything to do with the writing: to make it better, to learn the craft, or even the need for a place to show up with completed work, using the group as a de facto disciplinarian. And all this may be true. But ultimately we join writing groups because we are looking for safety and freedom — the freedom to be who we are without pretensions or alibis, and the feeling of being safe in expressing who we are. It is through our search for our own kind that we find a home for our heart. Within our writing community we connect with others of our own tribe, which opens us and ignites our spirit.

Groups provide a way of transcending our self-centered interests. Or, as British author and professor Bernard Crick put it, "The more realistically one construes self-interest, the more one is involved in relationships with others." In writing groups, we are with kindred spirits speaking a common language with a shared passion.

Groups nurture our self-esteem as writers. Here the writer is taken seriously, our work is treated with respect and so are we. People empathize with us, they understand and accept us and what we do, our opinions are listened to and valued, our intuition and creative process are respected.

Do a five- or seven-minute freewriting on your ideal writing group.

In groups we learn from each other and provide a safety net for one another. Lights get turned on in the shadowy areas of our writing and our lives that we didn't know needed illumination. Other participants reflect back to us what we need to know, especially if we come with an open mind and an open heart and if we trust the process. When self-doubt comes in on little cat feet, dragging home who knows what, a group can be a source of strength and healing.

This is the place to be when you're feeling stuck. Everyone knows the feeling and has a war story to share. There's nothing better than a sympathetic ear. Except maybe some ideas on how to get unstuck. Got a success to celebrate? "I finished a chapter!" "I got past that awful scene." "I got my first royalty check. $37.53." Say that to a family member and you might get hoots and jeers. At your writing group, you're more likely to be toasted with champagne. Who else cares or understands that your characters talk to you in the shower? Or that it took seventeen rewrites to finally get that one paragraph to say what you wanted?

Groups give us motivation and courage to continue. We don't have to go it alone. And besides that, we get to have fun together. How terrific to laugh out loud with other writers at the very thing that might have brought us to tears at home alone.

Writing groups nourish the hungry writer, provide salve for the wounds that must come if one is to surrender to her art. They teach us compassion and respect and encourage us to open our hearts to others and to be gentle with our own fragile being. Out of all of this comes a deepened capacity to understand what it is to be a writer.

Often as we delve deeper and deeper into our writing and our writing practice, we discover writing goals that couldn't have existed before we began the journey. Still, at any given time, we will have goals that we can identify. Before I found myself fifty pages into writing a novel, my goals would have been primarily about short stories and personal narrative essays. Take a few moments to make a list of some of your writing goals at this time, knowing they may well change as you continue your practice.

✓ Wants, Needs, and Intentions: A Checklist for the Writer Looking for the Perfect Group

Joining just any group doesn't serve either the writer or the group. For you to find the right group, you'll have to decide what is important for you, what your goals are for your writing and for the community the group provides. The following checklist can help define your wants and needs.

I want a read and critique group.

I want a group made up of my peers.

I want a group with a leader or instructor I can learn from.

I want a support group to share my writing with, not to be critiqued.

I want a group of like-minded writers.

I want a group writing in my same genre.

It's okay with me if group members are working in different genres.

I want a study group.

I want to work on a specific project with a group.

I want to develop relationships with other writers.

I don't have much time, so I need a group that meets...(fill in specifics).

I want an ongoing group that I can grow with.

I want a short-term group that I can work through my (project) with.

I'm not ready to commit to a specific project, so I want a group where I can fool around with my writing, try to get some footing.

I don't want to join a group, I just want to build relationships.

I want to practice my writing and expand my "voice."

I want to work on specific aspects of the craft.

I want a group made up of my gender (or other specific qualities).

I want a group that is diverse.

I want to write with a group on specific issues (gender, violence, body image, etc.).

I would like to start my own group.

I prefer to join a group that already exists.

I want to work within a large, established group.

I want a small, intimate group.

Add your own wants/don't wants/needs.

If you're not certain what you want, do a freewriting on what your ideal writing group would be. What you have to give to a collective and what you want to get from one. Imagine yourself at a meeting of your group. What's the setting? What's the focus of the group? How is the gathering structured? Who else is there? What's the feeling? How do you feel?

Make a list of your writing goals and then go through the checklist again.

Essentials for a Group Member

Groups are about relationship and begin with the most important one-to-one relationship, that of you with yourself. Following are the qualities that make a good group member.

- A healthy sense of self. More than just self-esteem and self-confidence, you need to know your strengths and limitations, and be willing to admit them. You need to be clear on what you want from the group, and to be able to ask for what you want if you feel you're not getting it. Your sense of self keeps you from the need to defend yourself or prove yourself.

- A desire to work with others and an interest in their work. Being a part of a writing group means giving and receiving, and who can say which comes first? We learn our craft by paying attention to what other writers do (and don't do). Be willing to share great parts of yourself, your thoughts, opinions, ideas, feelings, and concerns.

- Openness and flexibility. Any writing group will include others who will have their own opinions and ways of expressing them. Writing styles and approaches will differ (and thank goodness for that). Writers are a passionate group and strong opinions and viewpoints come from this passion. Diversity makes a group stronger, and tolerance underscores that strength.

- Willingness to work within the group's structure and guidelines. When we become part of a group — any group — we must be willing to surrender some of our independence for the good of the group. And to compromise. This doesn't mean a loss of personal integrity. For a person comfortable with her sense of self, being a member of a group doesn't threaten or take away; it adds.

- Willingness to take risks. Speaking your voice, even when your views are different from others, requires a willingness to step upon shaky ground. Being open to listen to others' views and opinions takes courage and an honest desire to improve. Reading your work aloud to others, listening to their critique, and giving your critique on others' work always involves taking chances.

♦ ♦ Quicklist: Essentials for a Group Member

- A healthy sense of self
- A desire to work with others and an interest in their work
- Openness and flexibility
- Willingness to work within the group's structure and guidelines
- Willingness to take risks
- Willingness to work through conflicts
- Willingness to practice skills that enhance the group
- Willingness to honor your commitments

♂♀ Techniques and Qualities for Individuals in a Writing Group

- Come with an open heart
- Come with an open mind
- Be honest
- Be compassionate
- Be respectful of the writer and her work
- Be concise
- Be specific
- Be direct
- Be kind
- Trust your intuition
- Listen
- Pay attention to non-verbal language
- Honor the creative effort
- Find something positive to say
- Be curious
- Speak from the heart
- Be thoughtful
- Maintain a sense of humor
- Forget personal agendas
- Set aside your ego
- Remember, it's the piece, not the writer
- Remember, critique doesn't mean criticize
- Don't speak too soon
- Don't talk too long
- Don't solve the writer's problems
- Remember to breathe

- Willingness to work through conflicts. Conflicts will arise as sure as a stretch of Midwest summer will spawn thunderstorms. Any group made up of creative, passionate people is bound to have conflicts about everything from the order of readings to the quality of food that's being served at the breaks. Resolving these disputes takes participation by all the group's members.
- Willingness to practice the skills that enhance the group. Communication, participation, honoring the work, respecting other group members' opinions, generosity and open-mindedness are some of the characteristics that will be called into play.
- Willingness to honor your commitment. When you join a group be certain you understand the group's purpose and ground rules. Know how much time will be required, and what you'll need to commit to beyond actual time in meetings.

Share all that you are. Your unique qualities and experience add to the richness and diversity of the group.

Taming the Beast — The Fears and Joys of Being a Member (and a Writer)

Even as much as we want to be part of a writing group, many of us suffer anxiety about joining one. We're afraid of making the commitment, afraid that maybe we're not good enough. We don't want to look foolish or be found out (that we can't write, that we're fakes, that our writing is mediocre or worse).

It's natural to feel some apprehension about joining any new group. Add to that the basketful of misgivings we have about our writing anyhow, and we can end up with as many doubts as plot twists in a good whodunit. How will we ever find our way home?

The first thing to understand is that we're not alone in our concerns. Most writers I know are insecure at best, anxiety ridden and angst filled at worst. And why not, this is a risky business, exposing ourselves in the permanence of black and white. It's good to know that experts say most of what frightens us isn't real. In one twelve-step program, old-timers tell newcomers that fear is an acronym for False Evidence Appearing Real.

"There's a voice inside our heads that's always heralding doom and disaster even before we get started on something," writes Dr. Susan Jeffers in *Feel the Fear and Do It Anyway.*

While it may be a waste of time to root around for the deep causes of our anxieties, it can help to identify such apprehensions. Calling something by its rightful name can take some of the power away. Also, when we break them down into their smaller parts, our fears don't appear as daunting as the whole black cloud of anxiety that rises on the horizon of our subconscious.

So, what are the fears of joining a group? Following is a brief list that other writers have claimed.

Fear of rejection
Fear of not being good enough
Fear of not knowing how (to critique, to write in a group, etc.)
Fear of intimacy
Fear of commitment
Fear of being disillusioned
Fear of finding out I can't write
Fear of finding out how good I am (not very many actually voice this fear, real as it might be)
Fear of failure
Fear of success
Fear of completing something
Fear of not completing something
Fear of being judged
Fear of being found out
Fear of reliving an uncomfortable or difficult experience
Fear of looking foolish

While it may be a waste of time to look for the deep causes of our fears about being part of a writing group, writing about the fears and calling them by their rightful names can take some of the power away and perhaps reveal information. Do a five-minute freewriting about your fears. Begin with "I'm afraid…" and don't worry about anything being "silly" or "petty." Fears come in all sizes.

➥

After you've completed your freewriting about fear, read through what you've written to discover any doors that need to be opened: statements that hold more inside than the words on the page reveal. Look for areas that arouse your curiosity or give you pause. It may be most helpful to write about those things that you don't want to look deeper into. The ones that make you cringe a little or cause you to blush.

Fear that I'll lose my voice (and I'll write like everybody else in the group)

Fear that I'll find out I don't have anything original to say

I tell my students that the anxiety that surrounds writing will never go away completely, we just get used to it. The same might be true about joining a group. You may have first-time jitters again and again. Maybe you'll have a pang of dread each time you have to read aloud or give feedback or critique to someone else. I know some longtime writers who have never overcome the anxiety of reading their work aloud. Others simply won't take the risk of writing spontaneously with a group.

On its own, fear won't disappear. And, the more you listen to it, the louder its braying becomes. If you're experiencing a little (or a lot) of misgivings about being part of a writing group, here are some strategies that might quiet the noise:

- Be gentle with yourself. Laugh at yourself, name your bogeymen and give yourself rewards when you are able to stick your tongue out at them. Take baby steps, just like writing — a word at a time. Go to a one-time-only group first. Try a drop-in group, where you don't have to make a commitment. Or join a group that lasts for only four weeks, or six sessions. Don't try to do it alone. Go with a friend. Ask if you can sit in on a group you'd like to join to see how it works.

- Go to an open reading and just listen. Read your work aloud to one other person. Start with a writing partner. Read your work into a tape recorder and play it back. Celebrate the sound of your own voice.

- Talk to yourself. Self-talk laden with positive messages can change fear energy into positive energy. Eliminate the *can'ts, shouldn'ts,* and *ought-tos* from your self-talk vocabulary. Say affirmations. Write them in your notebook.

- Use your imagination. Visualize yourself doing what you're afraid to do; see yourself as a graceful, strong, and capable member of a writing group.
- Get information. This is one of the best ways to conquer fear. Talk to other writers who are in groups. Ask how it benefits them, what they like, what the trade-offs are. Why they stay.
- Write down all the reasons you want to be in a group. Freewrite what you'll be like as a successful member of a group.
- And most of all, remember to relax and breathe.

On the flip side of fear is joy, and this is what writers I know say about the joys of being with other writers:

A great feeling of being connected
Finding out about my writing and myself
Fun of listening to other writers' stories
The experience of hearing how other writers do it
A sense of accomplishment at having produced something, finishing
The delight of finding out I'm good, that there is promise

When it's been tamed and domesticated, fear serves its purpose. It keeps us from strolling on freeways and scratching behind a lion's ears. In its most primitive form, it gives us the energy we need for flight or fight. And for us writers, it brings another gift. Like all emotions we experience, feeling our fear gives us more grist for our writer's mill. Use it.

A Place at the Table

The idea of joining an existing group reminds me of the old Groucho Marx line, "I wouldn't want to belong to any club that would accept me as a member." It also brings to mind a scene in a young adult novel

Rather than doing the freewriting exploration about your fears, make a list. Write as fast as you can as they come to you. Don't stop to think or consider what you're afraid of, just let the images come to you and write them down. Never mind if you repeat yourself. Sometimes the repetition emphasizes the weightedness of the particular anxiety. After you've created your list, choose one or two (or more) to do an expanded writing about.

"Find people whose spirit you enjoy; share your work, your heart and your dreams with them and you will have friends for life."

— Linda Watanabe McFerrin

being written by one of the members in my Monday night read and critique group. Debby's character Marissa is a thirteen-year-old whose mother up and moved them to Southern California, sans Dad. Like any adolescent, Marissa is caught up in the need to be a part of the group rather than being seen as the geeky outsider whom nobody likes. She joins up with a trio of girls she has nothing in common with and whose values are as far from her own as she is from her old home in Doleham, Massachusetts. Poor Marissa, she'd rather be a part of a group that fits like a bad training bra than eat lunch in the cafeteria by herself.

So it is with some of us writers who want so much to be a part of a group that we join one without knowing its values or structure and hope we can make it fit, or we join one we know isn't right for us because, well, it's better than being the lone writer at the geeks' table.

If you're invited to join a group, be clear on what you want and that this one will fulfill you. Don't join a read and critique group if you're still exploring your voice and you're uncertain of what you want to write. Or, if you join a read and critique group, be sure the participants are working at a level compatible with your experience. Look for peers and those who are slightly more experienced. Others' knowledge can help you learn, and you'll be stretched to go to the next level. A beginning writer with her first short story half-completed may not fare well in a collection of many-times-published writers. And, if you're writing nonfiction articles, you may not want to be in a group made up of playwrights.

So let's say you've been invited to join a group. Maybe you met another writer at a book signing. You both are wild about science fiction and you seem to have hit it off well. She tells you her group has an opening and invites you to drop by one evening to meet the others.

Here are some questions to ask yourself after the session:

- Is the group working on material and at a level compatible with my own work? How's the fit? Am I willing to give up, compromise? Stretch? (Go back to your "Wants, Needs, and Intentions" checklist, page 21.)

- Given that I had first-time jitters, did I generally feel comfortable with the group?
- Was there anybody in the group who absolutely turned me off?
- Did I sense a fire alarm go off or even a little pinging that sounds like the "door ajar" reminder in my car?
- Does the structure of the group fit my needs (meeting time, length, meeting place, the way the group is organized, how they tend to the work)?
- What about the general personality of the group? Compatible?
- Would I want to try again before making a commitment?

Making the decision to join might feel akin to checking out a new day-care center for your little one, or to use a more cynical metaphor, shopping for a used car. But a visit or two should tell you if this group is for you and whether it will support you and your writing. If you do decide to join, good for you. Adventures of all manner await you — from getting to know your new colleagues to settling into the feel of the new surroundings. Don't be surprised if you feel a bit the outsider for a while. Welcoming and friendly as the group may be, it still takes time to feel like one of the crowd rather than the new kid on the block.

Be open, lead with your heart, be honest, and be yourself.

On the other hand, what if you like the group, but they say no to you? Yikes. Talk about rejections. Best to view this one the way you'd look at a submitted story being rejected by a publication. Maybe you didn't do enough research before you sent it off; the publication (the group) wasn't the right one after all. Maybe your submission didn't fit their criteria (you're writing a novel; the group is working on short stories only). Maybe they had too many submissions (applicants for the group) and yours didn't make the cut. Could have been a bad day for one of the readers (group members); acceptance is so often subjective anyhow.

No matter what anyone says about not taking rejections personally, it's difficult not to. We're a sensitive lot, we writers. But just like

Take an inventory of the different groups you've been a part of — writing and otherwise. List the strengths and weaknesses, what you loved and what you didn't. Look for similarities and patterns. What role did you take on in the different groups? Always the same, or were you more active in some and less in others? How would you describe yourself as a member of a group? What are your individual gifts to a group?

having a piece rejected by a publication, don't let this stop you. As my friend Michael Hemmingson said, "The road to publication is paved with rejections." Either find another group to join, or start your own.

The Construction of Community: Start Your Own Group

Even if you've never been in a writers group before or attended any sessions, you can start one of your own. All it takes is the willingness to be a beginner, the courage to reach out, some planning and research, time (a little or a lot, depending), a measure of hard work, and finally, persistence. (Sounds a lot like writing, doesn't it?) If you're the kind of writer who's willing to undertake a start-up, first a few words of congratulations, then come the cautions.

It takes a special individual who will pick up the shovel and take the lead in breaking new ground. Someone with courage, which doesn't mean you're not afraid. It means that you're willing to go ahead in spite of the fear. Most of us writers want to be in groups and a good number of us need the support and camaraderie experienced writing groups furnish, but few of us have the courage or stamina to be the one to stage the party. Thank goodness for people like you who know the value of community and are willing to make the commitment to bring it about. You may be modest and say you're only doing it because you need the group yourself, that it's really selfish on your part, but we're not buying that. To all the community makers I say a big thank-you. And I know I'm not alone in my praise-singing.

Also, even in large cities with active writing communities, finding a group to join can be next to impossible. Your only option may be to take the initiative and start your own.

Before you set out with your pick and shovel, you might want to run through the "Wants, Needs, and Intentions" checklist on page 21 again to get a clear idea of what's important to you. Once you have your blueprints, you can begin to gather materials, and then it's on to the building stage. You may also want to see if you can attend a session or

"Thank goodness for people like you who know the value of community and are willing to make the commitment to bring it about."

two of some groups that are already up and running. Try to find those with varying structures and styles so you get an idea of the who, what, where, when, and how of it. However, if you can't locate any such groups or aren't able to sit in on any meetings, don't let that stop you. Just like writing a novel, you don't have to know how to do it before you set out. In fact, if some of us had known what we were supposed to do, we'd never have undertaken the thing to start with.

Often all it takes is two writers to get a group started. Maybe you have a good writing friend or know someone from a class or workshop who's also interested in starting a group. Like most other jobs, it's easier when you've got help.

If you're starting off completely solo, first thing to do is make a list of people you know who might also be interested. List writers from classes you've taken, from other groups, people you've met at readings or book clubs or in some of your various circles.

Ask people you know of others they know and keep expanding your list. Once you have a few interested individuals, invite everyone together to explore ideas. Maybe those who come will have more names to add to the list. At the initial meeting distribute copies of the checklist on page 21 and ask folks to complete it. Chances are not everyone who attends the first meeting will want the same thing. In this case, maybe more than one group will emerge and so much the better.

Other ways to find potential members: Put up notices at cafés, on bulletin boards at schools with creative writing programs, on-line (on Web sites or bulletin boards devoted to your city), in publications that offer free listings, such as alternative or neighborhood newspapers. Leave flyers at libraries, go to readings and announce that you're forming a group, ask the host bookstore if you can leave information. Give flyers to groups that are already formed, groups that might have similar interests, such as Artist's Way groups or book clubs. Be on the lookout for community gatherings where writers might be: book festivals, poetry readings, open mike nights at local cafés, Bloomsday celebrations, or Banned Books Week observances. Keep your literary radar turned on and tuned in.

♀♀ How to Start a Group: To-do List

- Recruit a writer friend to help
- Make a list of those who might be interested (from classes or book clubs, for example)
- Ask other writers for additional names
- Post notices at cafés and community centers
- Leave flyers at libraries and bookstores
- Spread the word at literary events, readings, open mike readings
- List in neighborhood newspapers, alternative publications
- Use the Web for local listings, local bulletin boards or e-newsletters
- Hold initial interest meeting (in public space)
- Keep the faith

(Note to established groups looking for new members: these methods can work for you, too.)

Don't be discouraged if your first attempts fall short of your dreams or if your group is small and wobbly for a while. Anything new takes time to find its groove. This is where persistence comes in. Many were the weeks I sat alone at a table with high hopes and sharpened pencil waiting for someone else to show up for my Brown Bag sessions, my scraggly notebook a beacon to all the like-minded ships at sea. Reread your list of "How to Start a Writing Group" to-dos and see where you can redouble the effort.

On the other hand, don't be too surprised if your efforts reap gold. No matter what the town or city or suburb, I'm certain you'll flush out other writers hungry for community. We're as common as sparrows.

And even if your initial group doesn't succeed, maybe one or two writers will find each other and form a partnership, or a group you never could have imagined will take wing and soar. Simply by lighting a single candle you may be showing the way for those who couldn't see in the dark.

Remember, every writing group started with the longing of one writer to connect with another. If you are that writer, then go for it. Who knows how long or far or wide your dreams can go?

"First we connect with ourselves, our love, power, passion, wisdom, feelings, creativity, then we connect with others."

— Charlotte Sophia Kasl

Moving On: When You Outgrow Your Group

Even though it seems we've barely started talking about being in a group, for a moment and for the sake of organization, let's move ahead in time to touch upon the occasion the might come when you're ready to move on from the group you're in. It's not about leaving town or (heaven forbid) giving up writing, you've simply outgrown your group. You're not being stretched or challenged anymore, the critique or feedback isn't helping you, or you need new voices, new faces, new points of view. Leaving a group can be a hard choice, especially when you've been with some of the writers for a long time, writing that first, second, third draft together, or meeting together each Tuesday at noon for more years (and more full notebooks) than you realized. Still, the time comes to move

on. A writing group isn't like a marriage. You didn't sign up "until death
do us part." No need to go to counseling or to try to work through
things. Leaving a group isn't like a divorce. Even an amicable one.

It could be that you just need a break (but not from your writing,
not ever from the writing), and after a sabbatical of a few weeks or
months, you can return. You may find a little time away is necessary to
refresh yourself and your writing.

Could be, while you're away, you'll discover you really are finished
with the group, but you've done it for so long it's become more habit
than choice, or you've been hanging on because you didn't want to "let
them down." You may feel disloyal, as if you are betraying family.

The most important thing is to be honest with yourself and true to
your writing. If you really do need a change, explain how you feel to the
group. Don't leave without saying good-bye. Take responsibility for your
own stuff and allow closure to happen. After you leave you may miss the
individuals and the community you've been a part of; expect some of that.
Being on your own may feel scary. Or to the contrary, you may have a
sense of possibility and excitement at what's to come. Either way, you're
on the road to a new destination. Another opportunity to grow, to move to
the next place in your writing and your life. Above all else, keep writing.

✓ Time to Move On? A Checklist

- You feel bored, stifled, and uninspired.
- You begin to make other plans and accept dates for the time
  your group meets, a time you've always held sacrosanct.
- You're not preparing a manuscript or giving the time or
  careful attention you always have to the work you take to
  sessions.
- You find fault with other participants. Their work and their
  personalities.
- You don't pay attention to the comments of others, or you
  disregard them or dismiss them with a "what do they
  know?" attitude.

- The meeting time or place has become inconvenient.
- You feel like you've "been there, done that" with the individuals and with the work.
- Seems like you're retelling rather than inventing. You haven't felt the creative edge against your skin in too long.
- The work is too easy. You could do it in your sleep.
- You don't sense your comments are helpful to others anymore. That you've said all that's to be said and you're tired of hearing your own voice.

3 WRITING GROUPS

Writing Groups 101 — The Basics

Imagine you're plotting ideas for a story or getting down a few of the details you want to include in a play. You might note something like: setting (small Southwestern town), time (mid-fifties, summer), characters (Josie, a woman rancher, late forties, widowed; Butch, her son, early twenties, hates the ranch and his name; Pelé, wrangler just arrived from Colombia, illegally), and so on. You'd set out the parameters and details that you knew at the moment (who can ever know all the details? There are always so many surprises), and dive into the writing.

This same exercise works for writing groups. Individuals who want to set up a writing group must begin with some sort of blueprint to work from. Call them guidelines, values, objectives, principles, or standards; those who will be a part of it must decide what the group is about, how it will work, and what's important to the group as a whole as well as to individual members. The sooner the ground rules can be set down, the better the chances of building a solid, lasting group.

Everyone knows values such as honesty, trust, open expression of feelings, and commitment to the writing and to the group are important, but don't they just go without saying? Well, no. Like in any relationship, those things left unsaid are generally the chasms that grow too wide to cross. If you don't talk about what matters to you, others are left to guess, and it's in the guessing and assuming that we begin digging holes. Values are intangible qualities and, like any other idea we writers try to communicate, we must wrap words around those things that can't go without saying.

Ground rules (call them guidelines if *rules* sounds too hard-line) can be developed within the first meetings of a new organization. Or, if your group's been around for a while and operating by the seat of your collective pants, you might want to discuss what's important to your group and write out a set of ground rules. "Oh, so that's why we keep running into that same sticky place." A few weeks after she'd read a draft of this book, my friend Lynne said her new travel writing group devoted a meeting to establishing guidelines. "We found the exercise of discussing these issues very illuminating and bonding for the group," she said. See sidebar on page 37 for a copy of the Compass Rose Travel Writers Bylaws.

Some ground rules that might apply:

STRUCTURE OF THE GROUP
> size (how many members)
> style/purpose (read and critique, writing practice, etc.)
> meeting times
> length of meetings
> place of meetings

PARTICIPATION OF MEMBERS
> punctuality
> attendance
> bringing pages and copies when it's your turn (for read and critique)
> come whether you have pages or not (for read and critique)
> participation in the workshop exercises or writing practice
> leadership or facilitator roles

DECISION-MAKING PROCESS
> how changes are made in structure or ground rules

NEW MEMBERS
> process for bringing in new members
> recommendation by a current member
> submission of writing

"…you have to keep close to people who see you as a writer. In this sense, new friends may be the best friends."

— David Bradley

"temporary" membership to see how the fit is, for the potential
member as well as current participants of the group
what to do when a potential member doesn't work out

Each group will determine its own ground rules, and to be sure, they'll change as the group matures or as new members join and the focus or interests fluctuate or the dynamics shift.

After three years of ongoing meetings, the leader of a group I participate in decided to introduce some attendance and punctuality rules. Attendance had become spotty and the energy was uneven. She said leading the group sometimes felt like "pushing a train." Another group had been using a book on the craft of writing fiction as the basis for its meetings, but after they'd worked through all the exercises a couple of times, they decided to toss the text overboard and chart their own course. Rough waters for a while, but soon they were sailing into a sunset of their own gorgeous design. A third group started off meeting every week, but soon members decided it was too often and opted for every other week. Conflicting schedules caused the occasional postponement and the constant rescheduling threw everyone's calendar into a frenzy. Finally, dates of the first and third Saturday of the month were set; you either make it or you don't. In my read and critique group, first this person then that one showed up without pages until at some meetings, there would be but a single manuscript to read. Our solution was to set up a schedule with sign-ups for specific dates to bring work. The act of signing up made the commitment more concrete and writers began to look forward to their obligatory reading date.

Have the group determine what it wants and try it out for a while. If it works, don't fix it. But if it doesn't work, change it.

"Keep away from people who try to belittle your ambitions. Small people always do that, but really great people make you feel that you, too, can become great."

— Mark Twain

Compass Rose Travel Writers Bylaws

1. The purpose of Compass Rose Travel Writers is to foster and encourage its members to develop their craft as travel writers,

become better writers in general, and (if a personal goal) to increase their chances of publication.

2. The group will consist of a maximum of ten (10) members. The group's e-mail list may consist of more individuals who attend infrequently or who wish to be informed of guest speakers and other special events.

3. New member recruitment is through referral by existing members. New member candidates are invited to attend up to three meetings as a guest, after which the group votes on whether to extend membership. The vote to extend membership must be unanimous.

4. Members will be dropped if they do not regularly attend meetings, fail to bring materials to read, do not critique in a constructive manner, or are otherwise disruptive during meetings.

5. Meetings are held from 6:30–8:30 P.M. every other Tuesday. Punctuality is important, both in beginning and ending the meeting.

6. Meetings are held in a member's home or a commercial meeting space that affords privacy for the group. The responsibility of providing/securing a meeting location will be rotated among the members.

7. This is a read-and-critique group. Therefore, members are expected to bring material to read at every meeting. Bring enough double-spaced copies for the group. Works in progress for critique are not to exceed 1,500 words.

8. On a quarterly basis, a guest speaker will be invited to give a presentation to the group. These meetings will be held in a private room at a restaurant. Invitations to these meetings may be extended beyond the group's formal mailing list to ensure the largest possible audience for the speaker.

9. On occasion, members will be given the opportunity to travel together on a day trip and/or overnight outing, write about the experience, and later share that work with the group so that we may learn and grow as writers from this shared experience.

10. Every six months comments will be solicited from the members (via e-mail) about the "health" of the group. These comments will be the focus of a meeting in which concerns, grievances, and suggestions can be discussed in an anonymous fashion and addressed in a constructive manner.

Steering the Course

In any gathering of two or more, the born leaders are bound to emerge. They can't help themselves any more than the sun can keep from rising. Also, something in the rest of us causes us to turn to them much like we turn our faces to the sun; we gravitate toward the light. This is the truth about authentic leaders: they lead so subtly and with such a fine touch, the rest of us don't feel led. It's as if we knew all along where we were meant to be and so we're not surprised when we arrive. The true leader is one who arouses the response of each participant in the group without asking, without telling and without giving orders. In *365 Tao,* Deng Ming-Dao wrote, "True leadership is a combination of initiative and humility."

There will be others who are not so much leaders as they are controllers; they have an idea of how things should be and they don't hesitate to tell everyone exactly and specifically, sometimes frequently and usually with a certain amount of noise, what they have in mind. These are the ones who cause uprisings and coups and mutinies.

Ideally, within a group leadership roles and responsibilities will shift. Different people will take on setting up the meeting room, maintaining the phone or e-mail list, communicating with other members, serving as timekeeper, and so forth. The formality or informality of structure will come out of the style of the group itself.

The facilitator's role is to maintain the supportive and respectful atmosphere of the sessions, to navigate the group through or past pitfalls and danger, and generally keep the train on its track. A good facilitator will sense when a distraction needs tending to and when the group needs to talk about an issue. She feels underlying tensions before they

"True leadership is a combination of initiative and humility."

— Deng Ming-Dao

have a chance to build momentum and is able to lead the group through the thickets to safe ground, not by sidestepping or circumnavigation, but through masterful path making.

A Dark and Stormy Night or a Tranquil Beach at Dawn: The Emotional Landscape of a Group

A writing group is a living, breathing thing that takes on a life of its own. Like any independent, individual entity, it has a unique shape and energy that are formed in many ways: through the individual members, the design and purpose, the physical setting, the aesthetics, the weather, even the day the group meets and the time of the session. Change any one element, and the whole thing shifts and readjusts and reforms itself. The dynamics of a group in January might be completely different from the same group in July. This isn't just so with writing groups; it has to do with any group. Theoretical studies abound on the psychological and sociological aspects of groups and group behavior. We won't go into all that.

Just know that within any given group, there will be highs and lows, difficulties and conflicts, passions and opinions, and maybe even boredom. Most important is that the group spends some time on its own well-being. Temperature taking and landscape adjustment may be needed from time to time. Individuals must be willing to speak up and talk about anything in the group that they sense is amiss. Saying what's working is a good idea, too. Like positive feedback on a manuscript, it reinforces what's going right.

It takes time for a group to develop its own personality and for participants to feel they belong. Trust isn't born in an instant; like a good novel, it evolves over time. As members begin to share and to recognize common experiences, understand and relate to each other, relationships are built and connections evolve. This thing called bonding happens. You may notice one day after a meeting, or maybe even in the midst of a particularly lively and spirited discussion, you suddenly feel a part of something important. It's a good feeling, this connection with community. It's what keeps us coming back.

♀

Typecasting Writers

Groups are made up of individuals and some individuals are more, well, individual than others. Scattered along the margins are some broad generalizations and personal observations on behavior and characteristics of writer types I've come to know that can affect the dynamics of a writing group.

We all come to a gathering toting our own bag of emotions. And, as the session progresses, certain events may trigger feelings on a group level or with individual members. Then there is the general emotional tenor of the group itself. All these play a constant and changing sound track to the meeting.

Maybe someone gets anxious about time running out, or nervous about reading, or, after reading, a writer might be rethinking what she said or focusing on what was said about her piece. Outside disturbances distract: sirens, dogs barking, someone shouting. I remember one workshop when we were interrupted by the passage of a parade on the street outside. Another time, someone in the next office made an emergency call to 911; we couldn't help but eavesdrop. Once there were gunshots!

Sometimes physical discomforts can get in the way of being present. The meeting is heading into its third hour and no one has moved from the chair they've been sitting in since they arrived. People are hungry. Or thirsty. Or the bathroom calls. Heaven forbid someone's cell phone rings. And she answers it.

All these distractions and occurrences affect the emotional landscape of a group.

On an individual level, if you feel yourself not being present with the group, one of the best ways to reconnect is by becoming aware of your body. Notice how you're sitting in your chair, roll your shoulders and stretch your neck. Change the position of your feet or legs. And remember to breathe. A few deep in-and-out breaths will bring you back into your body and ground you in the present.

Each participant is responsible for the well-being of the group. If one person notices emotions going wonky or senses that tension needs to be released, it might be a good idea to suggest that everybody take a deep breath or stand and stretch. A simple, "Does anyone else feel like we need to take a break?" is sometimes all it takes to bring the emotional gauge back to level. And when the inevitable conflicts flare, it's best to deal with them right away. (See "Tempests in Teapots and Other Containers" on page 47.)

We writers can be a volatile bunch. Sensitive, too. It's important to

The committed writer is an inspiration to the rest of us. There's never a question of what's important for this person. Writing. No matter what else goes on in her life, writing is the main event. She never complains about how much time it takes or how long the process. She is the passionate one. She believes in herself and her writing. Watch her, learn from her. Let her be your model and your guide.

✝

Maybe I'll write. And maybe I won't. Just the opposite of the committed writer, the tentative writer's art can depend on him about as much as an ice skater can depend on April ice. Apply no weight; it may not hold up under even the slightest pressure. Tentative is a difficult place to be. Without passion or commitment, tentative leaves a slightly dissatisfied feeling. Like the kid who goes to the refrigerator, opens the door and stares in. "I want something, I just don't know what." Make a choice. Take a stand. Be certain and bold and reach for those grapes with a greedy hand.

take care of our needs, discuss and process what must be dealt with, fix what should to be fixed, and then get on with our work. Remember, a community is a thing of value, worth protecting and nurturing. Tend to it with an open heart.

Qualities of a Good Group

Every well-run organization evaluates its performance. That's why grocery stores run inventories and cars have 45,000-mile checkups. A writing group should do no less. This kind of stocktaking offers opportunities to fix what might need fixing and to acknowledge what is working. And, though it may cause him to turn over in his grave, I'm going to go ahead and paraphrase Tolstoy. "Happy groups are all alike; every unhappy group is unhappy in its own way."

At least once a year and more frequently for newly established groups, set time aside to take an inventory. Open and lively dialogue is best, but some participants may not feel safe enough to voice their opinions — especially if the group is new or they are new members. A written survey can serve as well.

Make up your own questionnaire or use the following to evaluate the well-being of a writers group.

Do group members know and agree on the group's purpose and values?

Are your group's ground rules clear and understood by group members?

Are new members made to feel welcome?

Are attendance and participation regular and consistent?

Is there a frequent turnover of membership? Do members leave without saying good-bye or explaining why they're leaving? Or do they simply disappear?

Are leaders organized and well prepared?

Are people generally on time and ready to do the work?

Does leadership rotate or change?

Does the group get to the business of its reason for being? Or has a read and critique group disintegrated into a rehashing group? Has a writing practice group become a chitchat group?

If you could put a name to the emotional tenor of the group, what would it be (supportive, enthusiastic, passionate, lively, bored, lackadaisical, tense)?

Is there a feeling of trust and openness?

Does the behavior or action of one person ruffle the smooth feathers of the group?

Does the group take time to process anything that might come up that could cause problems?

Do people have fun as well as get the work done?

Is there a general sense of friendliness and support within the group?

If one member is having a difficult time, does another member offer to help (coach or mentor or work through something outside the group)?

Does everyone in the group take responsibility for the well-being of the group?

Does everyone in the group take responsibility for him/herself?

Is there spontaneity within the group?

Does the group meet the creative needs of its members?

Is there a general feeling of connectedness and community in the group?

It's been noted elsewhere, but there's no harm in stating it again like other old chestnuts we can't hear too often: The well-being of any group is the responsibility of each individual group member.

Show me a writer who isn't scared at least some of the time and I'll show you a person who is as out of touch with her feelings as a sociopath or as spiritually evolved as the Dalai Lama. We're writers, of course we're scared. That doesn't mean we don't write. Or rewrite. Or show our work to others. Or ask questions. Acknowledge the fear and move on. Light a candle. Say a prayer. Ask for help. Comfort and encourage one another and be kind.

Strengthening the Ties

A lively, well-built group has a foundation and structure that give it strength and participants who are committed and passionate; it tends to its affairs and nurtures and cares for its members. Beyond these elements, groups create and develop other activities that strengthen them and further bond members together.

As groups evolve, rituals may arise out of the natural procession of events. A certain way of starting each session with a reading of the guidelines or a particular quote or inspirational passage, such as Pablo Neruda's poem, "The Word." Maybe someone brings flowers each time, or a candle is lit, or a meditation spoken. Rituals are as natural to humans as eating. In fact, taking meals together has traditionally been a time and place where ceremony is invoked, and in some writing groups, the sharing of food is a significant aspect of the gathering.

Celebrations are another way of fortifying group members' ties. From completion of a first draft to getting a go-ahead from an editor, from acceptance of a poem to taking time away from a day job to go on a retreat, anything and everything that nurture and support and strengthen the writing and the writer are cause for celebration. So whether it's your group's tradition to applaud, give three rowdy cheers, or bake a cake, when members celebrate with each other, they're celebrating themselves, too, and their connection with each other.

If your group meets for just a few hours once or twice a month, going on a retreat can be an opportunity for members to spend more time together in a setting that inspires community. A weekend or longer away from the familiar meeting place and without the usual constraints of time and other distractions can deepen connections and encourage intimacy. Over the years, I've participated in a number of retreats that were as memorable in their settings as they were in their capacity for enhancing kinship. A long weekend at a cabin in the mountains, a getaway to a haven beside a mythic lake, a hole-up in a funky hotel with a hot tub and a mariachi band — all these opportunities for creating community added to my commitment to the group and my writing. I've also been to more than one retreat that started as a great idea but got twisted up into something more like a bad family reunion — like the one where there weren't enough beds to go around and one unlucky participant had to put pillows from the sofa on top of the pool table, or another where the only one who got a good night's sleep was the snorer

"The more you praise and celebrate your life, the more there is in life to celebrate."

— Oprah Winfrey

who was blissfully unaware that her all-night sawing rattled the coils in her roommates' bedsprings. And don't even ask about the mix-up with the menu assignments when we wound up with six bottles of wine and no chicken for the grill. Be certain everyone knows what to expect and what's expected, or your retreat might turn into a "get me out of here."

Meditation for a Writing Group

Meditation is a way of grounding and centering us. During the silence that surrounds the spoken words, we quiet the mind and become open to the "still, small voice" of inner guidance. The following meditation, or something like it that you create yourself, can be spoken at the beginning of any group's meetings. Where there are ellipses, pause and allow a few seconds of silence, then begin reading again.

Close your eyes and relax your body . . . let your body become comfortable . . . not rigid, but supported . . . stretch if you need to . . . roll your shoulders . . . roll your head on your neck . . . yawn if you want . . . and settle into a comfortable position. . . . Relax and let your thoughts go. . . . There is nothing to think about . . . no thoughts to hold in your mind . . . nothing for you to do or think . . . just breathe and relax. . . .

Notice your breathing . . . inhale deeply and let your breath come into your body . . . exhale and let the breath flow out . . . breathe deep into your lungs . . . and out again. . . . With each in-and-out breath feel the release of tension . . . follow your breath . . . inhale silence . . . exhale tension. . . .

As you continue to breathe in and out . . . listen to the silence . . . if there are extraneous sounds, let them flow through you on your breath. . . . Within the silence you may become aware of your body . . . you may feel your heart beat . . . you may sense the weight of your bones . . . and feel the chair as you sit . . . the floor beneath your feet. . . . As you breathe in and out in the silence . . . you are comfortable in your body. . . .

As you breathe in and out, let silence still your mind . . . thoughts may come and go . . . don't follow the thoughts . . . just let them flow through you until your mind is at rest. . . .

Somebody with a loud voice and heavy boots got to this writer somewhere between the formation of thought and the commitment of thought to page. Probably an old voice in her head that said, "Good girls don't" or "You can't say that" or "What will people think?" The censored writer is afraid of her voice, afraid of the power of her writing and afraid of being found out. Too often the righteous voice of the censor succeeds in shutting down this writer until she writes only safe, bland, vanilla-colored ambiguities, or worse yet, until she stops writing altogether because it is simply too dangerous. Encourage the censored writer to go deeper, to take chances. Do what you can to make her feel safe in the group and with her voice. Be a model. Sometimes the best example of how to take an uncertain step is in following the footprints put down by a more daring explorer-writer.

Here, within this silence, you are open to the wonderful mystery that is all creative writing . . . within this silent, safe place, you are surrounded and embraced by the bright light of creativity. . . . There is nothing here that gets in the way of the light . . . all shadows of ego and judgment and criticism are absent. . . . Here, there is only light . . . and you, as creator of the words and stories and poems . . . all that wants to be written. . . . Allow yourself to bask in this light. . . . Stay within the light of your writing for as long as you want. . . . This is your home . . . you are always welcome here. . . .

Now, slowly . . . gently . . . notice your breath again. . . . As you breathe in and out . . . allow your breath to bring you back from the silence. . . . As you breathe in and out . . . become aware of your body . . . and this room. . . . Take as much time as you need to return. . . . Slowly . . . gently . . . open your eyes. . . .

During the group's meeting time, the emphasis should be on the writing, but what a missed opportunity to be so focused on the work that time for conversation and conviviality isn't taken. I always look forward to the time my classes pass the four- or five-week mark. This is when I notice that some people start sitting next to each other each week, or smaller sets within the group go on break together. In the parking lot after class, trios or quartets of students gather in lively conversation; e-mail addresses are exchanged, and two or three individuals will get together for dinner before or drinks after, or attend a reading together. The whole atmosphere changes once these connections are made; we're no longer a group of strangers who come together for the class and attention is on the teacher. Now we're a community of writers with the easy exchange of friends and the class itself is only a part of what the evening is about. Trust is built as we get to know one another, and when trust is present defenses are lowered. Now we can really get down to the work.

Encourage communication outside the group, too. E-mail exchanges, phone calls, coffee/writing dates, carpooling to meetings, attending other events together. This camaraderie is as natural as wildflowers spreading their seeds; a few seedlings take root and before you know it the hills are covered in the bright blooms of friendship.

One writer is going to read at an open mike; everybody shows up. Someone's work is accepted for an anthology; the whole group is there for the publication party. One member attends a workshop with a well-known writer; she shares her notes with everyone. Someone sees something on-line or in a journal that he thinks his fellow writers would appreciate; he e-mails the URL for the Web site or makes copies for the next meeting. Need some help with a particular sticky spot and sense that one of the other writers knows more about it than you? Ask for help. One writer coaching another is part of the benefit of being in a group. At one time or another, everyone serves as teacher for someone else.

Tempests in Teapots and Other Containers

Put any two people together anywhere and sooner or later you can expect conflict. Some of us, in fact, can have conflict when we're in a room alone. Any group is bound to have occasional clashes, and when the group is a collection of passionate, creative writers, all the more chance for sparks to ignite.

There are those who say conflict is good. It indicates diversity and a difference of opinion and point of view. If there's no disagreement, they say, it means people are bored, that they're apathetic toward the group and its work.

In a writing group the content of a piece can light some fires and arguments can flare up over what the writer meant and what is the "right" view. When fictional characters are unlikable or downright repulsive, listeners may take it personally and challenge the writer. Sometimes writing offends and people react. A harsh or unkind criticism hurts feelings and anger is a natural defense. I've seen writers get hot when they feel someone has "stolen" their idea or image or phrasing. Judgments are made if one person thinks another isn't working hard enough or participating actively enough.

Conflict in a writers group, or any group, must be resolved;

♀♂ Strengthening the Ties

Community-making activities and attitudes that create a stronger group:

- Rites and rituals
- Celebrations
- Group dinners and gatherings
- Retreats and other group getaways
- Conversation and conviviality
- Communication outside the group
- Sharing other literary activities and events

"I'm not any good... it's okay, but... I'll never be good enough... This is just a little thing I started...My writing is just surface stuff...." The self-deprecating writer is the one who denounces her own value. Maybe she was taught it was not right to honor her own creativity or that people might think she was big-headed or is self-centered. Whatever the messages and however long ago they were told her (usually a long, long time ago), she still carries them around like a bushel to put atop her own light. Don't let her get away with that. Tell her how good she is, and invite her to say it. There's power in claiming yourself as writer and acknowledging your work as valuable. This is how self-esteem is built and esteem of the self is what it takes to hang in there with the work.

otherwise, like the mold on that square of cheddar you left in the back of the fridge, it will grow until the whole thing is clothed in the smelly blue velour of trouble. Issues left unsettled can lead to resentments, people avoiding one another, indirect attacks, subversion, and ultimately, the disintegration of the group.

Besides open confrontation, these are some of the signs that controversy has entered stage right: When the room goes absolutely and unnaturally quiet, not the kind of silence that follows a powerful piece of writing, but an uneasy quiet. If individuals fail to make eye contact or look tense or bored, or if someone sulks. Crying is a sure sign something is amiss; so is a person leaving the room in the midst of rising tension, or when someone clams up and doesn't participate. Body language speaks loudly, too. A defensive crossing of arms, a skulking down into the seat, leaning forward aggressively as opposed to eager anticipation. Clenched hands or jaws. Foot tapping, leg wiggling, finger tapping, lip chewing. And when participants miss meetings with no excuse or some obviously fabricated reason, there may be something else beneath the easy words.

When Trouble Rides In

Generally you can sense conflict in the air, or like a summer storm, you can smell it coming. See it heading over the horizon of bad manners or bad taste. Here it comes, riding on the shoulders of the person who wants to give too much advice, or the one who insists on trying to solve every problem for other writers, or tells the writer what he should have written instead of what is on the page.

Here are some of the behaviors I've heard group members complain about:

- Let's face it, they say, it's annoying when a person pontificates or natters on about whatever they believe is important whether it's on topic or not. And who wants to be around the person who's always the expert no matter what the subject or the guy who argues every point or defends every sentence? Nobody likes the soapbox oration, or listening to someone go on and on with as many details as a seven-year-old telling a plot to a movie.

- Want to stay in the group's good graces? Then don't be the person who brings twelve pages single-spaced when guidelines say eight, double-spaced and then asks for the group's indulgence. Don't come only when you have pages to read, or leave after your turn without participating in others' critiques. And please don't bring another rewrite of the same scene in which you've changed only a word or two in five pages. Bringing the rewrite once or twice is enough, then move on.

- Turn your cell phones and beepers off in session and don't keep getting up and down. Quit flipping through those pages and looking in your book bag for whatever it is you've got buried down there. Just settle down.

- Don't arrive late, come in with an entrance as big as Dolly Levi and disturb the group with your apologies. And don't be the one who always has some excuse to leave early. Groups need participants who honor the other members by sticking to the agreed-upon schedule.

Calming the Waters

Sometimes conflict erupts with the suddenness of a summer storm in the mountains and with just as much thunder and lightning. And, like a summer storm, it can pass quickly and without doing too much harm. Check the fences and rooftops. Make certain there's no lingering damage.

Other times trouble rides below water level, murky outlines in the shadowy depths, and even though they may sense its presence, no one is willing to look into the deep. This unacknowledged tension will ultimately find its way to the surface and what might have been an ordinary roller becomes a tsunami.

Each member of the group must be willing to intervene when tussles arise. And the best course is to intervene early, before trouble

Here's the writer who has all the answers for everybody else. Don't know how to make that dialogue work? Just listen to him; he can tell you. Wondering how to get your protagonist out of a jam? He's got an idea. Or two. And he doesn't hesitate giving them to you. Hey, he's glad to solve your problems. There's nothing he's afraid to tackle. If everyone would just listen to him, they'd know exactly what to do. "Why don't you make your main character a retired nun?" someone once suggested to me in a workshop. "A nun?" I said. Where'd that come from? Sure, and why don't I write a screenplay instead of a poem? The problem-solver is the distant cousin of the know-it-all and both of them come from a long line of egoists. Thanks, but no thanks, you can say. I like to work out my own knots.

No matter how you try to phrase something to this writer, he can't hear you. He's making too much noise defending what he's written. Or his way of writing. Or his idea, whether or not it made it to the page. This defensiveness comes from fear. In most groups, those who are receiving critique are not invited to enter into dialogue with the one giving the critique. You may have to remind the defensive writer of this rule.

escalates. Attending to areas of disagreement before they become real issues is one way of keeping the waters calm. Good for the person who can summon the courage to speak up when he senses tension in the room. Saying something like, "I'm feeling _____. Does anyone else feel that way?" Or asking a specific question to another person, "How do you feel, Rosie?" Just this brave toe in the door can make an opening large enough to allow others to enter into dialogue.

If the conflagration is of the sort that occurs when two individuals have clear and distinct and different points of view, others may have to sit by while each states her own case. If there's no resolution in sight, another group member may have to intervene. Maybe the two will agree to discuss their differences outside the meeting, or maybe they'll agree to disagree and move on. Much as we want to work through issues, a writing group is not a therapy group. The meeting may not be the time to process the differing perspectives.

If a major fission erupts that may be too hot to handle at the time, a few volunteers can meet outside the group to come up with solutions that the entire membership can discuss at a later meeting.

Groups can work through conflict with enough time and if members are willing to tell the truth. It also takes open-mindedness, an appreciation of diverse points of view, and willingness to compromise or change.

What to Do with the Bores, Whiners, and Thugs

Even groups with some sort of membership qualifications can sometimes find themselves with a single member whose behavior is so outrageous it threatens the structure of the whole thing.

The guy who tells the same sexist jokes again and again. Even when you tell him to stop, he insists on telling another, beginning with "I know you won't like this one, but . . ." Or the man whose story becomes more aggressively violent and explicitly sexual each time he reads and you get the sense that he's not writing fiction at all, but using the group for his own twisted gratification. (This really happened in a group I led.)

The woman who won't shut up but argues with everyone about every comment. The person who wants to use the group for therapy rather than writing. The gossip who carries stories outside the group and tries to set one person against another.

In addition to bad manners and bad taste, there are those individuals whose behavior is so inappropriate and disruptive, something must be done if the community is to survive. I've been a part of groups that have fallen apart because of the conduct of one individual. If no one intervenes, one person after another leaves until the only one left standing is the oaf who caused the downfall.

This predicament illustrates the importance of ground rules that address the problem before it arises, when solutions can be set forth outside the tumult of emotions. It also reiterates the need to confront conflict when it first shows its sharp teeth, before it has the chance to draw blood.

What to do?

Often in situations like these, before the point of conflagration, two or three members have already begun to talk about the problem outside the group. Maybe one or more will agree to speak with the person about his or her behavior. This may be best done outside the group so the individual feels less threatened or "attacked" by the whole membership.

One person agrees to be mediator while someone else presents the case. Always it should be stated in "I" or "we" terms rather than the accusatory "you." ("We feel offended when you tell jokes that are sexist or off-color," rather than, "Your jokes are offensive." Or, "I'm disturbed that I've been hearing rumors about Phoebe using Roxanne's idea for a short story," rather than, "You're spreading gossip." Or, "Some of us are feeling like we can't say anything about your work without your taking offense and arguing with us," rather than, "You're defensive and you talk too much.")

Detachment is the map to use and compassion is the road to follow. Always the person should be given an opportunity to hear how people are responding to her behavior and, if she wants, have a chance to talk with the whole group. However, if after a discussion or two, nothing changes, then the group can agree to ask the individual to

There are those who believe they are channels for the Muse and once the moving hand has writ, refuse to go back and change a line of it, or a word or a period or a comma. "Well, that's just the way it came out," they say with a superior little smirk. Far be it from me to say how work is inspired and what messages might come whence we know not. But for most of us run-of-the-mill, everyday sit-at-the-computer-and-bang-it-out writers, or pen-to-page toilers in the grapevine of the word, our inspiration is more a hit-and-run kind of deal. If we're conscious enough to be present and surrendered enough to listen to the intuitive voice, then what finally appears on the page may have some petal of real beauty and the smallest bone of unfettered truth among all the excesses and meanders. Our job is to root around in the mess of it all and find what comes closest to telling the truth and cleave language to the spine of our idea. And we're not always the best judge of that. That's why we need other writers. Why we need readers we can trust to tell us what they see and hear. And then, we need to be willing to listen and to make changes.

leave. Better to prune a single branch for the health of the tree than to allow the whole thing to be damaged, perhaps beyond rescue or repair.

After all this about conflict and trouble and troublemakers, it may feel as though starting a group or being in a group might be riding into dangerous territory.

Not to worry. Rather than the foretelling of certain doom, these are merely words of caution and some hints on what to do if . . .

Go forth with an open heart, great expectations, a sense of humor, and all the passion you can carry. Tuck in talismans for tolerance, patience, understanding, good will, and compassion. Remember, conflict is as natural as night following day. It can be scary and maybe difficult to find your way in the dark. But remember, too, that moonflowers open beneath the blackest sky and the jasmine that blooms at night releases the sweetest scent.

From Idea to Final Draft:
The Life Stages of a Writing Group

Every group moves through phases, not all predictable and not necessarily in a straight line. Generally, there are five phases for writing groups. I've used the metaphor of writers' phrases for the sake of illustration in the following broad-stroked and admittedly brief sketches of the life stages of a group.

One: The Idea

When the idea for a novel or a story or a play or an essay hits, what excitement we feel. Giddy and alive, almost like being in love. Oh, the potential. Anything is possible. So it can be with the first stage of a writing group. In the idea phase of a group, people connect with one another's dreams. Participants are gentle and kind to each other. However, during this early phase, the more quiet or shy members may be reticent to speak up so those who are more outspoken may have more influence on how the group is structured.

♦ ♦ Life Stages of a Writing Group

Stage 1: The Idea
Stage 2: The First Draft
Stage 3: Rewriting
Stage 4: Final Draft
Stage 5: Completion

Groups don't always follow a set pattern. Like our writing, they take on their own energy and life.

Two: The First Draft

This is when we're just getting it down. The story begins to unfold and the characters' voices and points of view emerge. In this phase, members must say what they want and need from the group. As characters and relationships develop, complications ensue. This is natural and, in a story, we would crank them up. But they don't serve a writing group. Some changes in structure, purpose, or ground rules may be needed.

Three: Rewriting

If the group is willing to face the problems with the first draft it can move into this stage. By doing the hard work of rewriting, which can be messy and difficult, members honor their commitment to the group and their dedication to their work. In the evolution of a group, rewriting may mean restructuring meeting format or schedule, or redefining membership requirements. Just like doing our own writing, groups may need to return to the rewriting stage a number of times.

Four: Final Draft

Now comes the work of polishing. In the group at this stage, the level of trust is high, the work that is done continues to serve the individual writers. The group has taken on its own life and members are committed at a deeper level. People speak up when they need to and rough patches are worked through. A tremendous sense of community and connection is present and individuals genuinely feel their participation in the group adds to the quality of their life and their work.

Five: Completion

To continue with the metaphor of writing, we could call this the publishing phase. Here's what can happen:

The group goes on, strong and viable for years, decades even. Or, it may be time to disband. Some of the founding members leave and the new structure doesn't have the glue to hold it together. Perhaps the original intention has been met and there's no compelling reason to stay together. Agreement is made that it was fun while it lasted, but now we're ready to move on to something else. Everybody learned from the experience and that knowledge will be taken along to the next project.

Some groups may never get to the final draft or completion phases. They fall apart during rewrites or don't even get beyond the first draft. Individuals are unable to make the commitment to stay in through the hard work of rewrites, or they may not like the way the story is shaping up during the first draft and don't see any point in continuing with something that doesn't work for them. Like our writing, not every idea emerges as a completed work.

It's important to recognize that groups don't always follow a set pattern. Also like our writing, they take on their own energy and life. But if individual members assume responsibility for the health and well-being of their writing group, more's the chance it can survive and flourish through any and all of the so-called life stages.

Earthquake or Erosion:
The Disintegration of a Group

No matter in what stage a group finds itself, specific events or attitudes can cause its disintegration— from the slow falling away of members to the big blowup whose fallout causes some to swear off groups forever. (So much the pity.) Following are some of the reasons groups don't last, and what can be done to prevent, heal, or restructure.

"An effective workshop is usually the result of a great deal of collaborative hard work."

— Sands Hall

- No clear purpose.

    From the get-go, the purpose of a group needs to be stated loud and clear. We're a writing group founded to support the fiction writer through the process of read and critique. We're a writing group with the purpose of providing a time and a place for our membership to learn more about the craft through writing workshops. We're the Tuesday Morning Backyard Writing Group, dedicated to supporting writers through weekly writing practice sessions; our purpose is to create community, to write together, and to celebrate our voices. When the purpose is so clearly stated, participants know what they can expect. If your group hasn't yet stated its purpose, now's the time to do it.

• Not sticking to the purpose.

When a read and critique group disintegrates into a social hour, or a writing practice group doesn't write but chats its time away, that may be its demise you see clouding the horizon. When a group strays from its purpose, it's up to individual members to speak up! Pulse taking and regular inventories can help. With the recommitment of groups members, it's never too late to get back to basics.

• Lack of commitment to the group.

It's difficult to maintain the energy you need to keep a group running when individuals are lackadaisical about their commitment to the group. We used to call this kind of behavior "flakey," and the person whom you couldn't count on was a "flake." Sometimes they show up, sometimes not. Sometimes they bring pages for review, sometimes not. They arrive late, leave early, and don't participate in the sessions. Groups need to insist on commitment as one of the requirements of membership. A flake or two within the ranks can make the whole group itchy. Solutions: determine a set number of absences during a year; when someone misses more than the agreed upon limit, they lose their membership in the group. Discuss the importance of being on time and staying for the entire session with those who ignore or abuse the schedule. Same with the idea of bringing pages for review and being involved in the activities of the group.

Sometime, maybe long, long ago, someone told this writer a big fat lie. Probably said something like, "You're not really cut out to be a writer," or "I don't think you have what it takes, kid," or "Maybe you ought to change your major to accounting." Or something worse. Something that so wounded the fragile psyche of this writer, she's still got tender spots. It could have been one of those so-called brilliant teachers who set fire to her manuscript or threw the pages across the room, or humiliated her in some other heartless manner. Even though there's still that yearning in her to write, she's skittish as a puppy who's been punished for his exuberance, and who can blame her. It's tough being a writer. Most writers I know are sensitive folks who need nurturing and kindnesses, not bullying and browbeating. We hurt easily and some of us never fully recover. Be gentle with this writer.

♀♂ The Disintegration of a Group

Earthquake or slow erosion, some of the reasons groups don't last:

- No clear purpose
- Not sticking to the purpose
- Lack of commitment to the group
- Lack of commitment to writing
- Failure to address problems
- Failure to resolve conflicts
- Disruption by a group member

- Lack of commitment to writing.

   A lack of commitment to writing is how some groups fall away from their purpose. If a group is formed around writing and members of the group say they are committed to the writing but no writing gets done either in the group or outside, then group members aren't "walking the talk," as the saying goes. Commitment is demonstrated by actions, not words. Once again, it may be time for a recommitment from everyone involved, or at the very least, reviewing the purpose of the group to determine if it still meets the needs of the members. Purposes can be changed or restated; maybe the group members will agree they want a support group rather than a writing group.

- Failure to address problems.

   Problems in a group are as a natural as dust collecting on a glass shelf. Keep the room dark enough and no one will notice the gradual, mote by mote, layering. But let a little sunlight come streaming through a window and the place resembles at home with the Addams Family. Suddenly everybody's sneezing and one wag has written "Wash me" across the glass. Taking the time — a little or a lot — to discuss problems when they first begin to collect will guarantee a well-cared-for group. Saying at the beginning of a meeting, "There's something I'd like the group to talk about. Can we set aside some time at the end of the session to discuss it?" can set the stage for dialogue. As always, it's up to each individual to speak up when he or she feels something needs attention.

- Failure to resolve conflicts.

   We writers know about conflict. In our work we make it up, then make it bigger. But in real life, writing groups or otherwise, letting the conflict build and build and build is not a good thing. Unless conflicts are resolved, and the sooner the better, they can cause the demise of a group. For more about conflict and how to resolve it, see "Tempests in Teapots and Other Containers" on page 47.

- Disruption (by a group member).

I have seen how a member can disrupt a group. One bombastic, outrageous explosion by one member of a writing group and, like any assaulted landscape, the community is laid to waste. Another way one individual can cause the falling apart of the whole group is through gradual wearing down, like a file against a piece of metal, stroke by abrasive stroke. The metal resists the irritation of the file until, ultimately, it gives way. Like the soapbox orator who goes on and on, boring the entire group with opinions, rants, and judgments, or the fixer who's got the solution to everyone's problem, whether a problem exists or not. Surprising how one individual can have this kind of effect on a whole group, but it happens. To find out how to intervene on these disrupters of community, see "Tempests in Teapots and Other Containers" on page 47.

When Members Go Missing

It never feels good when members drop out of a group, unless they are those disruptive individuals referred to above. When *they* disappear, we all breathe a big sigh of relief even though we may do it behind our hands so no one sees how lacking in compassion we are. But sometimes the good writers go missing. Maybe they are more sensitive than someone thought and an outspoken critique sent them away, maybe the behavior of one of the members just got to be too much, or they're having an especially tough time with their work — a bad case of writer's block, a disappointing rejection, an oversight — maybe something happened between meetings that no one else knew about. When one of our own goes missing, we need to send out the posse. Or at least make some phone calls.

As an individual member, if you're the one who's leaving, don't go without saying good-bye. Dropping out of a group without saying why

Some writers have their disappearing act down to a routine. They start a group, hang out for a while, then drop out. Or they enroll in a class, make four or five of the sessions, then they're gone without a word. You see them at workshop for a few weeks, and suddenly, they disappear. Who knows what happens to the drop-out and why they left. My theory fits the same frame as the one who never finishes. Maybe the writer didn't know how hard it was going to be to commit to a group and show up every time with work to share, or that there would be expectations and uphill grades, or that writing isn't always easy and being part of a group makes demands on you. I tell the drop-out the same thing I tell the one who never finishes: hang around. Stay through the first hard part and then the next. Acknowledge your tendencies to jump ship. And if you have to leave, tell someone you're going. At least say good-bye.

(honestly acknowledging why to yourself is most important) can result in feeling something has been left incomplete, dissatisfied, a little guilty, and will generally create more "baggage" to lug around.

If losing members is a regular occurrence in your group, it might be time to check under the hood, find out what's going on.

Profile: Alliance of Writers

Diana Guerrero started the Alliance of Writers when she moved to the small (population 8,000) resort community of Big Bear, California. She said she was starving for any kind of creative stimulation, and while the entire area has a good-sized writing community, there were "not a lot of people who come out of their cabins."

With a background in public relations, Diana knew what she was doing. To get the word out about the group she sent press releases to all the media and placed posters in key spots around town. Flyers went up on bulletin boards at markets, the post office, library, mail centers, and related businesses like the coffeehouses and bookstores. She used the Internet to communicate with writers groups in surrounding areas.

In the beginning the group met at a local coffeehouse but soon moved to a bookstore, where it is given an upstairs meeting space for its workshops. The group also uses the sitting area downstairs, where a cozy fireplace nuzzles up against the coffee bar. Perfect for those snowy winter months. The group meets every Friday morning from 10:00 to 11:30.

They are a diverse collection of writers who work in different genres, from novels to children's books to nonfiction. Membership is about writing, not getting published. "Mixed genre is working for us," Diana said. "Because we have such a blend, we don't get into the technical aspects, but we're good at resourcing and connecting people to other people."

The meetings are as varied as the membership: one week is a round-table, when participants discuss topics such as writer's block, how to get published, query letters, and other topics on craft. Another Friday features "feedback," which is what the group calls its style of read and

"…there's a camaraderie, the sense that you're with people who think like you do. It's nice to be among fellow writers who care about writing and how you suffer."

— Jean Femling

critique. Each member makes comments on manuscripts that are brought to the session, then the whole group discusses the piece. Participants can choose to get feedback in writing, in which case they e-mail their manuscript to the others before the meeting.

The second Friday of the month is reserved for guest speakers whom Diana recruits. If the guest is a published writer, the bookstore hosts a book signing for the author.

During each meeting a notebook is passed, and individuals write down their goals for the week. At the sessions, they go around the table and members say how the work went for them that week. Did they make their goals? Exceed them? Still working on it? "Writing down the goals is one of the favorite things about the meetings," said Diana.

Because the group is located in a small mountain community and, except for their own sessions, members don't have much opportunity to interact with other writers, they carpool to meetings of other groups or to hear special presentations. The town also has an open mike session run by a local poet and a creative alliance whose membership comprises a mélange of artists.

The Alliance of Writers — it's also been called the Writers Group of the Southern California Mountains, Writers Creative Cluster and Big Bear Writers Group — is still young; Diana started it in 2000. In the beginning about half the members had not been published. Now everyone has been published and one writer credits the group with helping her to finish her novel. Group members support one another however they can. And they support the group by making donations of "time, talent, and treasure," according to what they can give.

Diana continues to moderate the weekly meetings and to keep communication going via e-mail to all the active members as well as other writers she knows. Some weeks she puts in as few as two hours of volunteer time, other weeks as much as ten hours or more. She also designed and maintains the group's Web site and sends out press releases. At the first anniversary she sent out an announcement of the group's success. As a result two of the major publications "on the mountain" did features, which attracted new members. Now, she

"Nothing can encourage your dreams more outrageously than chums in mutual support."

— Patch Adams, M.D.

thinks, the group would continue if she were to leave, but in the beginning the strong and active leadership she provided was necessary for the group to get solid footing.

Diana started the group as a way to meet other writers and "to get out of the house." Now her goals have been met. The group is stable; participants are active and support one another. The small town is culturally enriched because of the exchange of creative ideas and energy and the synergistic start-up of other arts groups. The writing is getting done and writers have a community that provides a safe and nurturing atmosphere and a gathering place they can call home.

4 READ AND CRITIQUE GROUPS

Road Testing Your Manuscript

Possibly the most terrified look I have ever seen on a writer's face is during the moment she is about to receive critique on her manuscript. She's signed up for it, she wants it, she knows it is the next step and what is good for her and her work, still she is scared. Will they like it (me)? Will they tear it (me) apart? Am I making a fool of myself? (I'm making a fool of myself. I never should have said yes.) How bad is it really? (It's a mess. I'm a mess!) What on earth ever possessed me to do this? (Write. Come to group. Be born.)

And so, with fear in her heart and trembling in her voice, she begins to read her manuscript. Most likely, she reads too fast. She's not breathing, so her voice is getting squeezed out somewhere between the uppermost reaches of her chest and her throat. She reads very quietly (what if they really hear the words?) and maybe her hands shake. No doubt they are sweating and her heart beats so fast she can hardly hear the sound of her own voice, which is just as well; she would be embarrassed at its frailty. If she can just get through these next twenty minutes, she'll quietly slip outside, toss her manuscript in the trash can, and swear off writing forever. At least, writing that forces you to have an audience beyond your own scared self.

Now remind us again, why is read and critique important?

Read and critique is a way — possibly the only way — for writers to hear how their writing sounds to others. This is how we discover

"These fears, and others, are in fact commonplace, and one of the immediate benefits in joining a community of writers is precisely that discovery. Everybody is scared, everyone approaches the empty page with a mixture of dread and hope, and knowing this helps."

— Frank Conroy

whether what we scratched out on the page in our dim room under the waning moon, and fingered in, letter by letter, while the computer screen glowed silver against our slack mouths and glazed eyes, whether this piece we so painstakingly and painfully created and re-created works. Whether our crumpled ideas and manhandled images make any sense at all to anyone who isn't inside our own heads. God knows we've lost all sense of perspective.

Read and critique is how we regain that perspective. Or a new perspective that allows us to go further and into places we never knew existed. Sometimes what we didn't even know we knew appears on the page, but not until our fellow writers tell us it's there, do we see it.

How can we ever know whether that great idea we had (or so it seemed at the time) made it to the page unless someone else tells us? We are too close. We are inside. What we think is there may be there only in our woolly heads. Our subtlety so finely wrought, the thing we thought we were shaping with such sensitivity has disappeared completely. Not even a hole on the page where it disappeared.

"You're the first audience to your work, and the most important audience," said novelist Gloria Naylor. But, unlike members of our read and critique group, we can never hear it for the first time. We have written and rewritten and edited and polished and then started over so many times that nothing is new to us. Our objectivity gets amidst the drained coffee cups, crumpled candy wrappers, and chewed nails of our own review.

How is it possible that we could have missed the fourth repetition in two paragraphs of the word *orange?* What on earth were we listening to when we read the piece aloud and didn't even hear the same, boring sentence structure — subject/verb/object, subject/verb/object — pages on end? And where were the "was" police? And the cliché cops? That sliding point of view, that misplaced modifier, that clause as clumsy as a weary Santa Claus with an off-balance bag on a snow-covered roof at 5:00 o'clock on Christmas morning. How could all this have appeared on the page when it wasn't there at Kinko's when we printed out nine copies at two this morning?

Read and critique is the place where all this and more come to light. This is the place, among a roomful of trusted and supportive writing colleagues, where all the nits get picked and the warts exposed. And, if yours is a good read and critique group, you also get to hear from these objective colleagues what is working, where your digging really struck pay dirt, what new and exciting directions your piece can take. This is the place we get confirmation that we are writers and, never mind how much is left to be done, that our work has value.

✓ Why Read and Critique: A Checklist

Because you can never hear your work for the first time

Because you can never be totally objective

Because you lose perspective after a while

Because you can never know how your work will affect readers

Because reading your work to an audience changes it for you

Because different listeners/readers have different reactions to the same words

Because you can learn from other writers' reactions as well as their comments

Because it can bring up questions you didn't know to ask

Because it can help you pinpoint problems you sense, but cannot identify

Because your intuition will be confirmed and you'll learn to trust yourself more

Because it can help you to separate yourself from your work

Because it helps you develop your own critical sense

The perfectionist is the writer for whom nothing is ever finished, or good enough, or right. In worst-case scenarios, the perfectionist can't even get anything down. Perfectionism grows its pointy little seeds in the dirt of fear and has no purpose except to make us feel terrible about ourselves and anything we create. Here's the thing: perfect does not exist. We must make a thing as good as we can, and then release it and move on.

Contrary to rumors otherwise, and in spite of the bad, sometimes outrageous experiences of some, read and critique groups are *for* the writing and the writer, not against. In a good read and critique group, writers get substantive, concrete feedback on work in progress, encouragement to keep to the course no matter how disheartened or discouraged we may get, and support that we are doing the right thing. The

Like the committed writer, the passionate writer is sure of herself. Not only that, she's on fire with certainty. Ideas explode from her like hot spots from the sun. When she writes, she tears the paper with her enthusiasm. Her handwriting is bold, her strokes on the keyboard firm and sure. She's always ablaze. Maybe she doesn't sleep. Maybe she doesn't need sleep. Maybe she survives on her own fervor; she eats intensity and swallows the seeds. You can warm yourself on her energy.

thing we were meant to do. That is, write. When you leave your group, even if it's back to the starting gate for the whole piece you presented, you should feel good about the work and yourself. There will be a certain amount of release, too. Anxiety calmed by a stop at the nearest Ben & Jerry's or neighborhood pub. *Quel* relief!

Meanwhile, back to our writer who was last seen, voice shaking and palms sweating, at her first experience at read and critique. Now she's at her fifth or sixth session with the group. She knows everyone better. Knows who's going to listen for clichés, who's got the handle on characters, who knows language, and who cares about details. (Every read and critique group should recruit at least one Virgo.) Because she's been at this a couple of months now, she's better at critiquing her own work before she brings it for review. As a careful listener to others' writing, she has a keener ear for good writing, a sharper eye for what works and what never will. She's learned, too, what stones are always in the path of her own writing, and where the slippery places are. When she reads now, her voice rides strong above the fear that still accompanies such exposure. Maybe she'll never completely get over that sense of vulnerability that feels like moth wings fluttering at the light of her heart when she first reads a piece aloud. But never mind. She's more confident now. Actually looks forward to the feedback because she can see, in just these few months, how her writing has improved. Being part of a read and critique group has even made her feel more like a "real" writer.

Of course, not every one's experience will go as seemingly smoothly as this writer's. Throughout the next section, we'll take at look at what can go right and what can go wrong, with a few comments on how to steer the boat.

The Difference between Critique and Criticism Is Like the Difference between a Crystal Ball and a Wrecking Ball

We all know what criticism sounds like. Who doesn't have the voice of the critic skulking somewhere inside his head, usually hiding out in the caves of negativity, where the light never shines quite bright enough and the air is heavy with something going bad? This is the voice that says, "What junk!" (or worse) and finds fault with everything from your choice of words to your choice of toothbrush. "You should have got the hard bristles." Criticism finds fault, looks for what's lacking, condemns what it doesn't personally like or understand, which is well nigh everything you do. The Critic believes its job is to expose flaws, and if it can do so with a cruel wit and sarcastic tongue, so much the better. The Critic uses the work of others to show off its superior understanding of things and bemoans the death of anything really good or decent. The Critic is a righteous nag.

Critique, on the other hand, comes from a more generous place. At the heart of good critique are objectivity, honesty, and kindness. The role of one who critiques is not to use a jackhammer (or dynamite) to tear down a piece, then walk away from the rubble. It is to look at the construction, find what is strong and holds up the weight of the idea, and also, what weakens the structure. What adds to and what takes away. The voice of the critiquer is, if not gentle, then at least kind. There is a partnership between the writer and the one who critiques that is built on trust and respect. What is at issue is the work itself and each looks at it from as objective a point of view as possible — the critiquer most often more objective than the writer. This is to be expected.

The piece in question, whether it is a three-page scene, an eighteen-line poem, a three-thousand-word narrative essay, or the first or last or middle chapter of a novel, is what the exchange is about, not what the writer intended to write or how much the critiquer knows. It isn't about the writer's skill or where he's studied or whether this is his twentieth short story and fifteen have already been published. The dialogue concerns only what is on the page and how well it meets its mark or, if it doesn't, where, specifically, it veers off course.

I have heard unbelievably cruel and hurtful stories of critiquers who must believe themselves created from richer earth than the rest of us. A friend who had the pages of her short story thrown across the room by a workshop leader who said something like, "this is crap." Another writer who stared mouth agape while his teacher set fire to his manuscript. Then there's the instructor who thought it funny to tear the

The Difference between Critique and Criticism

- Criticism finds fault/Critique looks at structure
- Criticism looks for what's lacking/Critique finds what's working
- Criticism condemns what it doesn't understand/Critique asks for clarification
- Criticism is spoken with a cruel wit and sarcastic tongue/Critique's voice is kind, honest, and objective
- Criticism is negative/Critique is positive (even about what isn't working)
- Criticism is vague and general/Critique is concrete and specific
- Criticism has no sense of humor/Critique insists on laughter, too
- Criticism looks for flaws in the writer as well as the writing/Critique addresses only what is on the page

pages of a writer's essay in half. ("This is way too long," she said.) Someone else, a writer with a Persona to maintain, who took phone calls while participants, who paid a high price just to get into the workshop, never mind the weekly fees they anted up in addition to the entry fee, continued to read aloud. Oh, there are more. My own pages once dropped "accidentally" to the floor while the reader leafed through them, one imprinted forever with the dark shadow of his size fourteens, while he told me that "maybe I had a good idea or two, but . . ." You may have your own outrageous story to tell.

Who do these people think they are? While it may make for a juicy story, this kind of disrespectful treatment of the creative work of a fellow writer and human being goes down in my book as cruel and unnecessary. "Oh, I was glad he tore my pages up and threw them in the trash can, it showed me just how bad my writing was." Really? In my mind, we don't teach anybody anything by being cruel to them, or through disrespecting their work. Pompous behavior of this ilk comes out of ego and a need for power and doesn't have at its root honesty, objectivity, or kindness. I say, when someone treats your work or you in such a manner, you have every right, if to not punch them right in the nose, to let them know they are way out of line. If you can't get your money back, at least get your work back and get out of there as soon as you can. No one, no matter how many degrees he has, how much she's published, how many awards she has, or how much money he makes, has the right to treat another human being with disrespect. (Oh, have they forgotten their first attempts at transforming idea to page via language? I bet somebody, somewhere remembers.)

This is not to say that critique, honestly and objectively and kindly given, doesn't hurt sometimes. We writers are a sensitive bunch, how else could we do what we do? But our sensitivity comes with a double edge. In order to render the truth of the human condition on the page, we must feel all the pain, the loss, the heartache, the anger, the grief ourselves. And no matter how long we've been writing, when we tell the truth on the page, we have exposed ourselves and made ourselves vulnerable. You can't do one without the other. So when someone tells us

"No one, no matter how many degrees he has, how much she's published, how many awards she has, or how much money he makes, has the right to treat another human being with disrespect."

something isn't working, or wasn't as effective as we thought, or goes off the mark, it is as natural as tears to wince a little at the bruising. How tender we are. A speaker I once heard said, "I'm sensitive. I hurt easily and I don't suffer well."

All this said, more often than not, read and critique is a positive experience, especially when a group works together long enough to build a strong and trusted community, or when the workshop leader understands his job is to be objective, honest, and kind, and to support the writer and honor the work.

For those who've never participated in a read and critique group or taken a class where read and critique is part of the structure, it can take awhile to learn how to critique, and how to make the most of critique given. It may feel uncomfortable at first in offering your opinions on someone else's work. "I'm just learning myself, what do I know about critiquing what someone else wrote?" Further sections in this chapter speak to the specifics of what to look for and how to listen and offer how-tos, guidelines, and helpful tips. But like writing itself, mostly the learning will be in the doing.

Take One from Column A — Styles and Structures of Read and Critique Groups

There are as many different styles and structures of read and critique groups as there are sprinkles for frozen yogurt. Finding the one that suits your taste can be as haphazard as closing your eyes and pointing or as organized as starting with the almond slices and working your way through the white chocolate chips, lingering at the licorice, or dallying at the gum drops.

The primary feature of read and critique groups, besides the work done there, is that membership is almost always fixed. With the exception of special sections held at writers conferences, seldom are groups structured to allow drop-in participation. Like open mike readings, however, such meetings do exist and can be stimulating and diverse. They can be an evening's entertainment for the price of a cup of coffee.

In any group of twenty writers, there will be two or three without any learned skills or visible talent, only a desire to tell their stories; a few more with the technical know-how, but no passion; a half-dozen or more with talent, some skill and a desire to get better; maybe another five or six who, if they stick with it and one or two of them might, can reach a level of good to darned good. And there is one with the gift. Sometimes the one with the gift doesn't realize how good she is, or that she has been gifted. She may be full of self-doubt or insecurity or fear or confusion. But she has that rare gift of the natural artist. The thing is, she may not take herself or her art seriously. She may never rise to it. The brightness of it may scare her away. Ask her how she does something, but she may never be able to explain. She just does it. You may envy her and hate your black heart for feeling that way; jealousy among artists is as commonplace as grape jelly in Indiana. Instead, I say celebrate her, listen to her writing and glean from her talent all that you can.

Also, for those who want to get groups started, organizing and hosting a drop-in read and critique at a local café or a writer-friendly bookstore can be a good way to serve the community and help writers get connected with one another. But for the common variety read and critique group, the following notes apply.

Some groups are structured to have each writer read his own pages aloud, others ask participants to bring manuscripts that are taken home for review, then brought to the next meeting for discussion. Some writers like to have someone else read their work; other groups suggest a monotone reading so only the actual words will be heard, not a dramatic interpretation.

In some cases, participants get to read their work at each meeting, in others they get to read only twice a month, or once a month. Some groups limit manuscripts to three pages, some to five, some to eight or ten or twenty and some, no limits. Members hang in for the duration, which can be of some length.

Meetings can last from two to four or more hours, or, as is the case at the Southern California Writers Conference, some participants in the late-night rogue workshops find it a badge of honor to work six or eight hour shifts, reading and critiquing into the wee hours, until all the manuscripts have been read and only the hardiest are left standing. It's become a matter of reputation and, well, roguery.

Some groups limit their numbers to six or eight writers to ensure everyone gets to read every week or every other week. Others stretch the membership limits and choose who gets to read by lottery or some invented rotation.

There are mixed genre groups that invite writers of every style from cookbooks to children's books to participate, and others that focus exclusively on short stories or novels, even specific genre novels such as romance or sci-fi. Groups are formed to include all manner of poetry, or only narrative, only haiku, or "no rhyming allowed."

Like the toppings at a yogurt stand, there are advantages and limitations to every approach and construction. Some hold up for the duration of the cone, others slide off the side. Most important: that you find the

"...although in the end the writer is on a solitary journey, the writer is aided in ripping down the road by partnering up with trusted readers."

— Sheila Bender and
Christi Killien

group and the style that work best for you. As always, it helps to know what your goals are (do you want to publish? learn about other genres? be with your own kind?), how much time (and when) you have to devote to a group. If you've never been in a group before, it's to your advantage to check out a variety of already established groups. However, these can be difficult to find even in cities with large writing communities and a consistent source of literary information. You may just have to press ahead.

Following are some mix-and-match features for read and critique groups that you and your partners can use as you consider the structure for your own.

The Mathematics of Read and Critique

The size of a read and critique group will depend on the length of each meeting, how many participants read (and how many pages each), whether time is given over to the actual reading aloud during session, and how much time is devoted to each writer's manuscript. It's basic math.

Consider this: a manuscript page (double-spaced, twelve-point type, wide margins — see the sample on page 77) of about two hundred fifty words will take about two minutes to read aloud. So, an eight-page manuscript will take upward of fifteen minutes. The amount of dialogue on a page can make a difference — lots of dialogue, less time — and the density of the writing — long, ongoing sentences, no paragraph breaks, more time.

If the group allows a minimum of fifteen minutes critique for each reader in addition to the reading time, at least half an hour per person will be needed. In any given two-hour meeting, you should be able to read and comment on the eight-page manuscripts of four writers. Give or take. The take comes from the transition time between readers and the occasional piece that simply requires more than fifteen minutes to give adequate critique. Plus diversions into general discussions, questions that arise, time for breaks. Depending on the size of the group, not every participant will be able to speak on each manuscript. It may simply take too long.

If manuscripts are distributed ahead of time and individuals review them outside the meeting, more time can be devoted to critique, but the

It's a wonder even the first paragraph got written, let alone the first chapter. This writer is so intent on getting it right she's penned in by infinite rewriting. Writing, then rewriting, then rewriting the rewriting until the piece is as flat as a noodle and just about as bland. How can you rewrite when you don't even know what the story is? I ask. My advice to the rewriter is the same as to the researcher. First write the story, then make it better. Once you know what you have to say and what the story is about, then you can set about honing it to its purpose. Look for streaks of perfectionism in the compulsive rewriter. Suggest to him that he just keep moving forward. You'll walk along with him.

♀ ♂ Basic Questions for a Read and Critique Group

- How many members?
- How often to meet?
- How long to meet?
- How often do members get to read?
- How many pages of manuscript?
- How much time devoted to each manuscript?

writers (and the group members) won't have the advantage of hearing the work spoken aloud. Also, in a gathering of eight people, if each has ten pages of manuscript, that means each person must read and review up to eighty pages of work before each session. This can be daunting, especially if the group meets weekly. At one conference I attended, we were required to review two manuscripts for each day's workshop — eleven manuscripts in all (not counting your own.) In addition to the intense conference schedule, I had to critique up to forty pages each day. I was exhausted! And sometimes, reviewing my students' papers of up to sixty or eighty pages in a week throws my own writing way off track. So, this word of caution from a sometimes weary reader: don't overburden yourself with too many pages to read. You could find yourself resenting the work and those snide remarks that you thought you were only dark thoughts in your mean little mind might sneak their way into your critique. You want to always come at someone's work fresh and open and full of enthusiasm.

In read and critique the work is so intense and requires so much concentration that sessions of longer than four hours (eight manuscripts of up to eight pages) can be exhausting. That last manuscript may get the same kind of attention given the relish dish at a Thanksgiving dinner when the idea of a dill pickle seems just one mouthful too many.

As for the order of reading, I've heard writers say they don't want to be first because it takes the review of one or two manuscripts for individuals to settle into the work. Others don't want to go last because they believe the level of concentration has gone the way of the empty popcorn bowl and everyone is ready to go home. Such a quirky lot, we writers. Superstitious as gamblers and sensitive as a sunburn. Relieve some of the tension by allowing the reading order to be a playful start to the meeting. Drawing straws, rolling dice, or highest dollar-bill poker hand can get the session off to a lively start. At one late-night read and critique I ran, the rolling of dice got way too complicated and took too long for the fifteen or twenty of us involved. We were headed into the first half hour before we'd even determined who got to go first. Next night, we drew numbers instead.

With all this said, here are some basic points to consider for your read and critique group:

How many members?
How often to meet?
How long to meet?
How often do members get to read?
How many pages of manuscript?
How much time devoted to each manuscript?

Again with the Steering

Like croutons in a salad, leadership finds its own niches and people take on certain roles as readily as they choose cheddar over garlic. Some are natural managers who can keep a crowd of kindergartners or a pack of dogs on track; a group of seven writers is a slam dunk. There are communicators who remember when someone said they'd be late for a meeting and who's gone to Cleveland for a week. Organizers who recall the order in which everyone read for the last four meetings and who's coming up first three weeks from now. Bless the cookie bakers who can't help but bring goodies to each gathering. Always though, when it comes to responsibilities, it's best to err on the side of organization than to allow casualness to lead to chaos. Establish ground rules and commitments at the get-go and you'll be more assured of a smooth road no matter what the territory.

Certainly, you'll need a timekeeper to keep the critique and dialogue within time constraints that have been agreed upon. And to move the group along when things get hot and heavy or bogged down as they're wont to do. How is it we got sidetracked into a debate about which theater has the best popcorn or which was the decade of the wedgie? Never mind. Let's just get back to Janie's manuscript.

Finding a Home

Where a group meets can be as important as how frequently and for how long. As often happens when a new group is forming, one or

Once at a reading I gave, a woman asked me if I thought ten years' worth of research would be enough and should she start actually writing her novel now? "Ten years?" I asked, not certain I had heard her right. "Ten years and three trips across the country," she said. There was a touch of pride in her voice. The compulsive researcher is the one who can never know enough about her subject or have enough material to do it justice. If she ever does get around to actually writing, she'll be so stymied by trying to work in every piece of research that any story will be crowded out by facts. Write the story first, I say. Then do the research.

two members might volunteer their home. This arrangement can work well if the location is convenient for all, if the space feels comfortable and safe for everyone, and if alternatives are easy to come up with when the host goes on vacation or his day job keeps him at work late, or like the group that arrived on time for their 6:30 meeting, and their hostess who was still out shopping didn't lock her door. When she walked in with armloads of groceries, they didn't even break stride. Just kept on reading.

A note of caution: inconsiderate group members who leave behind a mess for the host to clean up, or a sink full of dirty dishes, or crumbs between the sofa cushions can turn a warm welcome into a cool get lost. Group members who want to hang around after a meeting when the host has other plans can also lead to irritations that, unless tended to, can grow into resentments.

Meetings held in public places can also have complications. Too noisy and the reader can't be heard, too quiet and the reading sounds like the Voice of God. Too many strangers around (in a café, for example, or at a bookstore), and the readers or critiquers don't feel comfortable or safe.

Renting a room means collecting fees and paying rent. Using someone's office or the community room in a public building is an option. Rotating meetings from one member's house to another can balance out the commuting distance and give every one who wants a chance to play host. Don't forget fine weather opportunities like meeting beneath a big shade tree in the park or outside seating areas in public places. Could be a nice change. Good for keeping the goings-on lively and stimulating.

Mixed Genre versus Focused Genre

Check out the different sections in your local bookstore and it becomes obvious how many ways there are to tell our stories. We writers come at this craft from many directions. Determining how many points on the compass you want to include should be part of your group's ground rule structure.

"We find a home for our heart when we are safe and know our voices will be heard."

— Charlotte Sophia Kasl

A mixed genre group invites participation by writers of all styles. Fiction, both long and short; poetry; creative nonfiction; personal narrative; essays; articles; memoir; autobiography; children's stories; and all manner of other writing.

This style has its drawbacks. Writers may be asked to critique what they don't understand or aren't interested in, and writing in some genres calls for very specific architecture. The well-meaning comments of one or two critiques can send a writer down the long, wrong road and coming back might not be easy.

On the other hand, writers get exposed to a wide variety of work and styles and can broaden their general understanding and hone their critiquing skills. I've been stretched by learning to critique everything from young adult novels to science fiction and fantasy and true crime. None of which I generally read or have studied. And, until I had grandchildren to whom I could read stories, it had been a long, long time since I'd looked inside a picture book. It helps if the writer can provide specific information that might be helpful in the critique. "In a children's picture book you can only use x number of words, and generally (this) has to happen." Or, "In sci fi, the writer has to create a whole world so..." Or, "In romance novels, the protagonist must meet her love interest by a specific page."

However, especially in small towns or when the writing community is limited in size, it's often either mixed genre or nothing. Two or three novelists might be scraped together, or at least writers of fiction, but pity the more rarified writers of stage plays or haiku.

A limited mix can work better than an all-genre group. For example, a collective that includes long and short fiction, memoir using fiction techniques, and creative nonfiction that borrows elements of fiction. Generally in these instances, participants are working with the same techniques, or at least within the same boundaries, using some of the same tools. For example, my Monday night read and critique group includes writers working on short stories, a memoir, a literary novel, a young adult novel, a mainstream novel, a story cycle based on autobiographical material, a "cozy" mystery, and a creative nonfiction book

"As one voice among many, I try to help writers give themselves permission to do what they've come there to do: to come into their own power as writers and human beings, to tell their stories in their own ways in their own voices."

— Lex Williford

made up of personal narrative essays. We do fine together, all of us getting better at critique and broader in our experience.

Focused read and critique groups — all novels, for example, or only short stories — can concentrate on a specific genre. But even within fiction writing there are dozens of styles such as literary, mainstream, mystery, thriller, and the so-called genre fiction: sci-fi, fantasy, romance, historical romance, action-adventure, and on and on. Each group gets to determine how wide or narrow they want their focus to be. Too narrow and you may lose perspective — all eyelashes and tear ducts — too broad and nobody knows where they are — some vast and distant space where there's no road home.

Whatever mix and match your group decides upon, remember that open and ongoing communication about the health and well-being of the group is crucial to its vitality. Just because you started in one direction doesn't mean, with discussion and agreement, you can't head off in another. There will be bumps in the road, detours along the way, and you'll have to stop to refuel from time to time. Don't forget to look at the scenery as you go.

At a Read and Critique Session

It's your turn to read. You've distributed copies of your manuscript to other members of the group. You've got your own copy, and your pen to make notes to yourself as you read, water bottle at hand. Everyone settles in and you begin. You may introduce the piece with a note or two of information: "Pete is the protagonist, Lily is his sister, their mother is Glorianna. This scene takes place about three weeks after their father was killed in an avalanche." And that's it. No mention of what you hope to accomplish in the scene, no explaining of Pete's low opinion of his sister's choice of boyfriends, or her previous attempt at drug rehab, no comments about how the mother and father got along before Dad took off on a mountain climbing trip with his guru, Ibid. What must work is what's on the page. If the listeners have questions or need clarification, they'll make mention of it in their critique.

"You don't stop in the middle of a sentence and say what you meant to write instead of what's there."

You begin to read. Your voice is loud enough so everyone can hear clearly; you read slowly enough that they can follow along on the page and make notes as you go. You don't read in monotone, but neither do you dramatically reenact the scene. You don't stop in the middle of a sentence and say what you meant to write instead of what's there. Even if you feel dreadfully uncomfortable when you get to the part that you realize doesn't work at all (how could it have sounded so good last night when you read the scene aloud for the fifth time before you finally went to sleep at 1:30 in the morning?), even when you feel the slow, red crawl of embarrassment scale your neck and head for your cheeks and suddenly it's so hot in the room your shirt is sticking to your back and the pages of your manuscript are curling from the sweat of your hands. Even then, you don't stop reading. You just remind yourself to breathe, keep your voice steady, and keep reading. Somehow you make it through the rough patch, reach the safety of an especially well-crafted paragraph, and head into the finish. Now you can stop, take a drink of water. Fan yourself with the crumpled remains of your pages and wait.

For some, this is the hardest part. To wait quietly and patiently while the other writers make their messy and lengthy notes all over the manuscripts you just paid way too much to copy at Kinko's. Nobody says anything. Nobody looks at you. They just keep to their scratching and scrawling. Someone's turning the page over to write even more on the back. Someone else is drawing great sweeping lines through whole paragraphs. The quiet is not unlike the time following that incident at the dinner party with your boss when you made that embarrassing faux pas about his new hairstyle and didn't he look just like Sean Connery when he finally got a new hair piece. In fact, waiting for the comments from the group, you relive that whole terrible incident, even down to how you dribbled wine down the front of your silk blouse, which never did come out completely.

You ruffle through your pages, making notes, and you can hear the whistle of your own breathing, which sounds like an F4 practicing touch-and-gos. This may not really be the longest moment of your life,

"After all, in offering a piece of writing one is really asking on an emotional level, Do you love me?"

— Gary Eller

not compared to, say, the time you had that growth removed from your back in an outpatient clinic by a surgeon you'd just met who reminded you of an ex-lover you treated badly. But this moment is a long moment and you have begun rehearsing your apologies for taking up the group's precious time with your own shallow, benign, banal scribbles, when, finally, thankfully, someone begins talking.

"Well, I like this piece, generally, Tessa. You've got a lot of nice tension going on that carries through to the end of the scene. And I really like the dialogue between Pete and Lily." (You breathe a sigh of relief so powerful it blows the napkins off the table.) "However. . ." and so begins the round-robin of critique. "This is working, this is not. I like this because. . . , I got a little confused here. I wasn't sure what you meant here, this transition is a little jumpy. . ."

And it continues. Each of your colleagues offering in clear, straightforward comments his or her individual and personal critique of your piece. They are objective, honest, and kind. Some of the concerns you had about certain sections are born out; your instinct was right again. Maybe someone even has a suggestion as to how it can work with just a tweak here or a twist there. Comments are specific as well as general; they take in the smallest nit of the piece and the whole grit of it.

The other group members have marked up the pages using notations and symbols that were agreed upon as your group's lexicon. (See the sample marked up–manuscript on page 77 as the beginnings of a lexicon your group can develop.) They've attempted to keep their handwriting clear and easy to read, though this can be difficult when trying to make notes and follow the forward motion of the reading simultaneously. When someone agrees with what another person has said, they don't repeat the critique, but acknowledge that they agree with So-and-so. This way you get a feeling of consensus when it's there. Or conflicting takes when it's not. No one asks questions that might require lengthy explanations; only those that can be answered with a brief yes or no. Otherwise the critique can veer off into a general discussion, and the point of critique is to address what is on the page.

"In writing workshops, you can express your deepest concerns in a forum where people are willing to hear you and willing to let you hone your expression."

— Molly Peacock

View From the 17th Floor
Workshop 5/11

She had another flying dream last night. She's had them since she was a *[Who? Give her a name.]* girl in Iowa, soaring above green hills, her shadow bumping along the tops of corn fields. Looking down from that high, free place, seeing the shape of her body rolling along with the Mississippi, <u>wide and flat as a noodle</u>, banking its *[Not clear — her body or the river?]* gentle turns, arms outstretched. She has always wanted to fly.

The wrought iron railing of the balcony comes just to midpoint on her rib cage. She holds onto the redwood trellis of the (bouganvilla) *[SP.]* to climb up. *[No para.]*

Balanced on the thin edge of the railing, she leans against the stucco wall for a moment, its rough texture leaving little indentations in her palm like a code. *[# para.]* The thermometer mounted on the wall measures sixty-five degrees *[① use of semi-colon?]* early yet, the sun is just beginning to warm this side of the building. There is a sweet coolness to the wind <u>blowing across her face.</u> *[Cliché. Make fresher.]*

She looks down, suddenly aware of her shoes — little white slip-ons she picked up at macy's *[caps.]* summer sale, satiny on the outside, an Oriental design *[nice detail]* embroidered in jewel colored thread. Pretty, she thinks, glad she's wearing them. Then, opening her arms in what might be a benevolent gesture to the city spread out below, she leans forward and falls into a graceful swan dive.

Isobel isn't a big woman, only 107 pounds, so when the updraft catches her, <u>it swirls her housecoat around her and lifts her up.</u> She's above her *[a bit awk.]* apartment for a moment, hanging there. The roof of the building a flat rocky expanse with air conditioning units squared off against each other, a faded red ball cap lying upside down like a bedraggled bowl open to the sky.

The air on her skin is light as a lover's kiss in the morning, as God's greeting. Welcome Isobel, come in, ⊗ [God says graciously.] He will open the doors *[don't need attribution.]* of the kingdom for her like some (gracious) host of a grand hotel. Not that Isobel *[repetition]* is leaping to her death. This (was) not suicide. *[tense]* The dive off her balcony is something else, though if she dies at the end, then she dies at the end. And doesn't it always come to that anyhow.

"All the successful groups I know also are strict about keeping the critique brief, and implacable about silencing the author. Adhesive tape is usually not necessary."

— Ursula K. Le Guin

During the critique, you remain silent. You make notes of the comments in your notebook or on the back of the manuscript, along with who made them, so you can ask questions later if you need to. Every now and again, someone takes up time picking one of those nits of spelling or the use of a cliché, or a line edit. But ideally those things are simply noted on the manuscript and discussion is devoted to larger issues.

Both Patty and Barbara agreed with Glorianna's presence in the scene. They thought her monologue added a great amount of tension to the meeting of brother and sister. But Paula said she thought Glorianna was too much and took away from what needed to be a confrontation between Pete and Lily. Frank said he never liked Glorianna in the first place, and every time she shows up she throws the whole thing off balance and maybe she should have her own story. Then there's Steve, who points out that this scene is the same scene that you wrote before only with Pete's other sister, and did it really need to be done twice. Barbara thinks your language is beautiful and tells you so.

At one point Patty and Barb start off into a side discussion about the competition that always arises between brothers and sisters, and Frank, who has seven siblings, wants to join in, but Paula, who's acting as timekeeper for this meeting, brings them back to point.

Five other writers, five different opinions about the work. Who's right, who's got a point, and who's so far off base they must have been listening to a story of their own making? You've been copying down notes furiously covering the backs of three manuscript pages. You can't remember the last time you breathed.

Finally, everyone has had his or her say and you wonder if you can ask a question. And since there's a bit of time left, you can. A few moments of lively discussion follow in which you get an idea of how you can use Glorianna's outburst to allow Pete to reveal something he knew about his father that even she didn't know. That will jump-start the next scene, and you gather up all the copies of the manuscripts with their notes and comments, which you'll review later when you've had a chance to get a little distance and eat some nice macaroni and cheese to soothe the rough edges of anxiety-induced hunger.

For now, it's on to the next manuscript. You take a drink of water, try to clear your head of your own work, what was done and what must be done next, so you can be present to listen to the next writer's piece and offer your own thoughtful, objective, and honest critique.

And so it goes, around the circle. Six group members, six manuscripts read. A little over three hours have gone by in what seems like but one. You'll all come together in two weeks and go through the process again. During that time you'll review the comments on the pages, maybe input some of them on a corrected and edited manuscript. Or transfer them to one complete copy that will contain all the notes and comments. Maybe you have a loose-leaf notebook where you keep all these, or a file cabinet, or a cardboard box on the floor of your closet. Maybe you bundle them together with a hefty rubber band, or after transferring all the comments onto a single copy, you put the used pages in the box of recycled paper that you'll use for rough drafts over the next week or two. You may or may not take the time to rewrite the scene now; it depends on whether you'll be able to continue moving forward if you don't rewrite. You agree with many of the comments, and appreciate the notes.

You notice that Paula always makes the same kind of comments about Glorianna, so you make a note to yourself to ask her about it. Maybe the two of you can go out for a coffee together and you can ask about her take on your character, and maybe, as has happened before, the two of you will delve deep into the kind of dialogue that only writers care about. Your discussion might go into a second cup of coffee. She'll tell you about the book she's reading in which the writer does some subtle layering with character and relationship. You'll get to talk about a recurring problem you have with characterization. Maybe, by the time you get to the shared chocolate mocha cheesecake, you'll have some fresh insight and the name of a new book you want to read. You and your friend have deepened your relationship by sharing what matters to you. And instead of dismissing her comments because no one else seems to feel the same way, you've uncovered a contradiction from earlier in the story that only she picked up but she hadn't been able to articulate.

What to Do with Critique

1. Let the critiqued manuscripts sit for a few days to cool off.
2. Review comments on the pages and the notes you took during the session.
3. Transfer comments to a master copy of your manuscript.
4. Select which comments to incorporate in the rewrite and which to let go.
5. Rewrite the piece now, or put away for rewriting later.
6. Save and store all the critiqued copies of the manuscripts, or
7. Recycle the paper by using the clean side for rough draft printing.
8. Remember to say thanks to your read and critique partners every now and again.

The next day, just like every other day, you'll return again to the blank page and do what you do best: Write.

The How and What of Critique

Critique is an opportunity to hear your reader's voice. The feedback you receive will tell you how your writing is being perceived by the listener. Mind you, in a read and critique group, the reader/listener is another writer, which isn't usually the case when we send our writing out into the world. Then we have lost all control of who reads it at what pace and how much attention is paid. At least, in read and critique groups we are among friends and colleagues. Everyone coming together over the next little bit of time with the objective of making the work as good as we possibly can.

Many beginning writers, or writers who have never participated in read and critique, aren't certain what to look for when critiquing a manuscript, or how to critique. Following are broad areas as well as specific examples of a few of the hows and whats. Writers can use the information when reviewing their own work as well.

- Be honest, objective, and kind. Tell how the piece affects you as a reader.
- Respond only to the work being read, not the writer's previous work, the writer herself, her hairdo, or the company she keeps.
- Critique the elements of the craft, not the content. The writer is the only one who can say what he wants to write about, and, ideally, he will write about what matters to him, what he is passionate about.
- Be specific in your comments.

Not just "I like..." or "I don't like..." Look for a foundation on which to base your critique. Also, move away from your personal opinions of like/don't like to what works in the writing and what doesn't work.

Elements of Critique

Voice

Voice is the way the piece is written — language, diction, rhythm, etc. There is the voice of the work itself, and the voice of individual characters within it. A writer will also develop a recognizable voice. Voice is what differentiates a story by Annie Proulx, for example, from a story by Gabriel García Márquez, an article by Barbara Ehrenreich from an essay by Louis Lapham.

Is the voice fresh and unique? Is the voice consistent? Is it appropriate for the work? Is there sufficient difference among characters' voices, or do they all sound the same?

Tone

Tone is the attitude of a piece — friendly, colloquial, formal, distant, foreign, exotic. It's how the narrator tells the story or the writer relates the nonfiction.

Is the tone established at the beginning? Is it consistent? Is it compelling? Appropriate for the work?

Language/style

Language has to do with voice, but it also has to do with the style of the writing. Writers must work all their lives to develop a language with which to tell their truth.

Is the language vivid? Clear? Fresh? Concrete versus abstract? Does the language get in the way or does it enhance? Are there "too many" words? Is the writing too dense? Or too sparse? Is the language repetitive or boring? Does the language fit the setting, tone, and theme?

Does the writer use figurative language such as metaphor, simile, imagery? Does she do it well? And do these complement the story?

What about the use of details? Are they relevant? Do they serve to reveal character or story or place? Too many? Not enough? Does the writer use sensory details to bring the reader into the story through the physical body?

What about style? Is it consistent? In keeping with the context of

Eight Techniques from Jack Kerouac

- Blow as deep as you want to blow
- Write what you want bottomless from bottom of the mind
- Remove literary, grammatical and syntactical inhibition
- Write in recollection and amazement for yourself
- Struggle to sketch the flow that already exists intact in mind
- Don't think of words when you stop but to see picture better
- No fear or shame in the dignity of your experience, language and knowledge
- Write for the world to read and see your exact pictures of it

the piece? Is there variety in sentence structure and paragraph lengths? What about the rhythm of the writing? Does the structure fit with the action taking place? With the emotional content?

Nine Guidelines from William Strunk Jr.

- Choose a suitable design and hold to it.
- Use the active voice.
- Put statements in positive form.
- Use definite, specific, concrete language.
- Omit needless words.
- Avoid a succession of loose sentences.
- Keep related words together.
- In summaries, keep to one tense.
- Place the emphatic words of a sentence at the end.

Diction

Diction is the choice of words, how a writer says something or how a character speaks in internal or external dialogue. One can be formal, the other colloquial. One proper, the other casual. The key is consistency and appropriateness, both with the tone of the whole thing and with the individual characters as well. An eight-year-old child won't speak in an English drawing room voice and an English baron won't use slang or colloquialisms.

Characters

Are the characters believable? Do you care about them? (You don't have to like them, but you must be interested in them.) Are they well drawn, with depth and color, or are they flat, one-dimensional, trite? Can you see them physically?

What about motivations and actions? Consistent with what you know about the characters? If not, do their inconsistencies add to the movement of the story?

Point of view

Point of view answers the question, "Whose story is it?" This is the voice of the narrator of the story, who is usually the protagonist. Generally, point of view is first person (I), third person (he/she or the character's name), or omniscient (often referred to as the "voice of god" because the omniscient voice speaks from every character's point of view, knows every character's thoughts). There are other points of view as well and any good book on craft discusses any and all permutations and the advantages and effects of each.

In read and critique, the important thing about point of view has to do with consistency and appropriateness. Is the point of view right for the story and is it consistent throughout?

Dialogue

Does the dialogue sound real? In keeping with the character's voice, the character's emotional state, and the emotional tenor of the scene? Does the dialogue add to the scene, the relationship, the movement of the story, or is it unnecessary? If the writer is quoting real people, does the dialogue serve the piece? Offer credibility or reveal character? Dialogue in nonfiction often does the same job as dialogue in fiction.

Setting/time

Every narrative is set in a place and at a time. As a reader, do you know where you are in the piece? Is it grounded in place? Do you know when events take place? Is time handled smoothly (flashback, compressed or elongated periods of time)? Does the setting add to the mood/theme?

Plot

Does something happen? If nothing happens, there is no story. As a result of what happens, does someone change? If no one changes, there is no story.

Did you want to keep reading? Did the story compel you to ask "and then what happened?"? Is there tension and conflict? (No conflict, no story.) Is something at stake? Does the story begin where it should, or are there unnecessary paragraphs/scenes/chapters? Does the thing diverge off into subplots that go nowhere? Meanders that serve no purpose?

Is the plot predictable? Or does something unexpected or fresh occur? Are there holes in the story or does it all hang together?

Structure

Think of structure as the architecture of a piece, what holds it in place and holds it together. Does the structure fit the narrative? (Would a short story be better suited as a novel? Does personal narrative work better than an article?) Is the structure built in an organized way? Does the logic hold together?

Twelve Suggestions from E. B. White

- Place yourself in the background
- Write in a way that comes naturally
- Work from a suitable design
- Write with nouns and verbs
- Do not overwrite
- Avoid the use of qualifiers
- Do not affect a breezy style
- Do not explain too much
- Do not take shortcuts at the cost of clarity
- Make sure the reader knows who is speaking
- Do not use dialect
- Revise and rewrite

Conflict/tension

In her book *Writing Fiction,* Janet Burroway says, "Only trouble is interesting." Every story, every narrative, every poem and play and article and essay must contain tension otherwise there is no compelling reason to read it. Even lighthearted humor pieces will contain some element of conflict. Otherwise: boring, boring, boring.

Does the piece contain conflict (two or more opposing forces)? Does tension result from this conflict? Does the writer keep the tension going or does he back off? Is the conflict believable?

Compelling or predictable/fresh or trite

Is this story new to you or have you read it before? It may be the same basic "plot" (boy meets girl, etc.), but is it told in a new way? Does the essay or creative nonfiction piece cause you to look at something in a different way? Do you want to keep reading to find out what happens next?

Transitions

Are the transitions smooth? Or do you get lost in time/setting? Does the writer bring you along through time/space?

Beginning/middle/end

Are you hooked from the beginning? Does the work actually start at the beginning? Does the middle keep the pace or does it drag or get bogged down? Are you satisfied with the ending?

Arc

In fiction an arc can refer to both the shape of the story and the transformation of character. Does the story curve up into a high point of tension — the crisis — then fall away into resolution so that the arc is conflict, crisis, resolution? Or is it flat? Does the protagonist change as a result of what happens in the story? Is the change evident? Believable?

Nonfiction will have an arc, too. From the beginning promise to the ending payoff, is the reader taken from here to there?

Seven Beacons from Gary Provost

1. Brevity
2. Clarity
3. Precision
4. Harmony
5. Humanity
6. Honesty
7. Poetry

Pacing

Is the pace of the writing in keeping with the pace of the story or piece? Are there parts that drag? Do you notice a place where you stop listening or your attention wanders? Are there other parts that seem to be skipped over, like stones over the surface of a pond? Does the writing move too fast when you want to linger, go deeper? Or move too slowly when you long to move forward? Pay attention to your feelings as you read, listen to their responses.

Theme

Theme is what the story or piece is about. It is not the "moral to the story," but the aboutness of the piece. Theme is embedded within, rather than laid over the top like frosting. Is the theme clear? Are all the elements of the piece consistent with the theme? Do they add to the unity of theme?

Research

In a nonfiction piece, is the research complete or does it feel sketchy? Does it add ground to the piece in accuracy and truth? Does the research interrupt the flow of the piece? Is there too much information/background?

Authenticity

Do you believe the writing? Is the writer being honest? Do you feel like you've been told the truth or a little ripped off or manipulated? Like a fine meal, are you satisfied at the conclusion, or are you left wanting?

✓ Elements of Critique: A Checklist

Voice
Tone
Language/Style
Diction
Characters
Point of View

Eleven "Fumblerules" from William Safire

- No sentence fragments.
- It behooves us to avoid archaisms.
- Also, avoid awkward or affected alliteration.
- If I've told you once, I've told you a thousand times, "Resist hyperbole."
- Avoid commas, that are not necessary.
- Verbs has to agree with their subjects.
- Avoid trendy locutions that sound flaky.
- Writing carefully, dangling participles should not be used.
- Kill all exclamation points!!!
- Don't verb nouns.
- Last but not least, avoid clichés like the plague.

Dialogue
Setting/Time
Plot
Structure
Conflict/Tension
Compelling or Predictable/Fresh or Trite
Transitions
Beginning/Middle/End
Arc
Pacing
Theme
Research
Authenticity

Keep your critique to what's on the page. Critique the elements of the craft, not the content. Be specific. Be honest, objective, and kind.

Preparing a Manuscript for Group Read and Critique

You prepare a manuscript for your read and critique group much as you would a manuscript you were submitting for publication. Big, wide margins, clean, easy-to-read type, double-spaced with lots of room for comments. The object is to make the reading easy on the eyes of the reader: editor and critiquer alike.

Here's what you do.

Before you even think of printing, run the piece through your spelling checker one last time. Then read it again. The spelling checker will let a wrong word through even though it may be spelled correctly. After you've printed one copy, read it aloud a final time before you print additional copies. There's always one last change you'll want to make, or a misspelled word or punctuation faux pas to correct.

Set your document format for:

Spacing: Use double-spacing

Margins: Wide margins (allow 1.5 inches top and bottom, 1 inch to the left, and up to 1.75 inches to the right. Set ragged right, rather than justified or centered, and flush left.

Page numbers: Either bottom right, bottom center, or top right. Number in Arabic, not Roman.

Header (that slug line at the top of each page): Include the title of the piece and your name.

First page: Title centered, about one-third down the page. (If you're working in scenes or partial manuscript, no need for first page title; use header.)

Typeface/size: Easy-to-read, traditional font set in "normal" mode at twelve point. Courier is still the favorite of some editors. Times Roman, Palatino, New Century Schoolbook, or a sans serif face such as Arial or the classic Helvetica. Do not use fancy, decorative, or script typefaces. Do not use italic or bold settings. (Of course, italic can be used for emphasis within the manuscript itself.)

Word count: Approximately two hundred fifty words per page (except the first page, which, because of the amount of white space before and after the title, will naturally be fewer). Note: Even if your group's maximum page count is eight, and your piece runs twelve, don't use a smaller font size or squeezed margins or half-spacing to fit. Either break the piece apart and read it in two or more sessions, or ask if you can bring more pages.

Paper: Basic white bond paper. One side only. No colored or decorated paper. Some writers prefer a "newsprint" stock of recycled paper; some like to reuse old manuscripts or other paper and print on the blank side for workshop use. We writers must take responsibility for all the paper we use and be conscious of both our consumption and waste.

Paper clip: Upper left corner. You may think stapling might make the thing more secure, but it's easier to handle loose pages than fold over stapled ones. Sometimes very large workshops or seminars will request manuscripts be stapled in the left-hand corner so pages won't get pulled out or lost in the shuffle of hundreds of submissions. But for general read and critique groups (and always for submission — except novels and other lengthy manuscripts), use paperclips.

Title page: For read and critique groups, you won't need a cover or title page.

Profile: One Day at a Time Writers' Group

The One Day at a Time Writers' Group got started the way countless other groups begin. A couple of writer friends wanted to get together to review their writing with each other. But two writers do not a group make so they set about to recruit other members. Both the "founders" were women in their fifties: Dian, a longtime novelist-in-practice and poet with a graduate degree in creative writing, and Judy, a start-again, stop-again fiction and nonfiction writer with a career history in commercial writing. They'd met in a book group and discovered their mutual commitment to writing and their desire to be in community with other writers.

Soon they found Julien, who wrote narrative nonfiction and had been published in the local alternative press. He knew Karen, a novice who wanted to write a nonfiction book about her experience working with at-risk babies. Ray, a sometime poet who wanted to try his hand at fiction as well as narrative nonfiction joined the group, and a playwright, Steve. Six writers. Enough for a group, albeit disparate writers of varying experience and different genres. Could be interesting and, all agreed, fulfilling. And with enthusiasm and high hopes, they came together and began to organize themselves.

At the first meetings, they determined their ground rules: they'd meet once a week — on Thursdays — at one of the members' homes. Two hours weekly. Three people would bring manuscripts, up to ten pages, with copies for all participants. This alternating week schedule would allow everyone an opportunity to read and receive feedback at least twice a month. An easy rotation was agreed upon; if someone had to miss a session, someone else would read. Because of the size of the group and friendships already established, informality was the dress code

"For the first time in my life I was around people like me — devoted to the twin acts of reading and writing. . . . For many years I had taken writing very seriously, but now I took myself seriously as a writer."

— Chris Offutt

of the group, but that didn't mean the commitment was informal. To the contrary. Some of the participants were looking to publish, some weren't certain what they even wanted to work on, let alone whether they wanted to publish, but most of all, they were committed to their writing and to the idea and ideal of a writing group.

Over the next few weeks, as the participants came together with their stories and narratives and poems, they grew more comfortable with each other's writing and each other's style and the process of read and critique. The group's statement of purpose and ground rules were agreed upon, typed up, and distributed.

Before long, the playwright, Steve, dropped out and Susan, who wrote fiction as well as nonfiction, was invited to sit in for a few weeks to see if she and the group were a fit. The idea of a trial period of a month for new members was proposed so that both the new writer and the current members would have a chance to try each other out. (Usually in peer groups such as this one new participants are invited to join by someone who knows them and can determine if they'd be a good fit or not. But, being a friend is different from being a member of a community, so having the escape clause of a tryout period in the written ground rules is a good idea.) Membership stayed steady for a few years. Meeting places changed as people moved from house to condo to house again. But wherever the group met the coffee was always hot and fresh and the writers were always eager to read their work, despite the normal anxiety that accompanies any first reading of new material, and to hear the work of the other members. Like moss on a shaded tree, trust grew rich and green and the writers began to take more chances in the work they presented, writing material that grew riskier and came from a deeper place. Some tried genres they hadn't worked in before, others dropped defenses and moved out of the head and into juicier stuff, where truth is closer to the bone.

They attended a few readings together and once, took their material to an open mike at a local café. They learned from each other, from their own writing and from the process of listening closely, paying attention and giving thoughtful critique to others. Over the years, some

"Like moss on a shaded tree, trust grew rich and green and the writers began to take more chances in the work they presented."

pieces got completed, others were published, and still others were abandoned. Or filed away in the bulging drawer with other unfinished work. Surprisingly — or maybe not, some groups go on much longer — the core group stayed together for more than three years and continued the writing and their commitment to community.

The last to join was the first to leave. Susan's personal life situation changed and she needed to focus her attention elsewhere. Then Karen, who was writing the nonfiction book about crack babies, decided to work with a mentor rather than stay with the group. The four remaining members continued to meet until two took on a major commitment that interrupted their ability to maintain the weekly schedule, and the group disbanded. One of the two men slowly let his writing drift away and another signed a contract to cowrite a nonfiction book that later saw publication. Dian searched out a new community and once again turned her focus to novel writing. Judy continued her writing, but didn't maintain steady membership in a group until a number of years later.

Of the original One Day at a Time writers, only the two original members continue to write and participate in writing groups as a way of life. But during the tenure of the group, essays, articles, poems, personal narrative, parts of books, and all manner of stories were worked on by writers and readers alike. A cooperative and collaborative feeling developed within the group and individual members and their writing flourished in the nurturing community. Knots in both writing and psyches were worked through. The writing got better and the writers more confident of themselves and their voices. Pages and pages of writing were completed and for those three years, the writers were connected in a way that only such a community can connect.

5 WRITING PRACTICE GROUPS

The Muse Works a Crowd

Of the many things an individual can do in the company of others, writing may be one of the few things that must be done alone. Right? Eugène Ionesco locked in his basement at his own request; Toni Morrison holed up in her single hotel room, shuffling another hand of solitaire. Poor Proust in his cork-lined room. Here's our writer, feet stuffed into shaggy slippers, a holey cardigan tossed over hunched shoulders, she's alone and alone, working into the night, working in the cool silver glow of her monitor with only her dictionary, her stamina, her small imagination.

Writing in the company of others might be all right for classroom exercises or avant surrealist experiments, maybe some airy-fairy New Age outdoor camp fest, but Real Writers, they have to go it Alone.

Or do they?

The old idea of the writer as solo artist is as outdated as the belief that you can't make jam out of jalapeños. Writers can and do write in community. And they write good stuff. I know. I've participated in writing in real-time groups for more than a decade and I've led my own twice weekly writing practice groups for nearly as long. This is what I know: On any given day a writer can write the best he's ever written. He can also compose a piece that's clunky and misshapen and downright embarrassing. Just like when he's alone.

I know that the people who participate in these groups are often

✐ Sixty Writing Practice Prompts

Following along in this chapter are 60 prompts for Writing Practice sessions. The prompts can be used for fiction or nonfiction writing. You can write about yourself (in the first person "I") or use the prompts to give voice to your fictional characters. When the prompt uses a pronoun such as "I" or "she" or "he," feel free to change it to anything else. Let the prompt suggest the writing, no need to follow it literally. And don't think about what the prompt means, just let the first image that appears in your mind be your cue to simply begin. Remember, there's no wrong way to write from these prompts.

remarkable writers who paint word pictures, spin intriguing and complex tales, and take great risks. These are courageous writers writing in "real time," making it up on the spot and getting it down on the page. During writing practice groups, prompts are given and from these few words, stories and poems and essays and scenes from novels get written right then and there. At least first drafts that flare up wild as prairie fires or emerge soft as twilight in September. Seeds are sown, characters appear (and disappear), ideas take root, and notebooks get filled. Something else happens, too. A certain and electric current of connection, not just one writer to another, but one human to another.

We come together for real-time writing or writing practice because we have experienced the collective energy that occurs when we join, with writing as our purpose. Some call it the creative force. Magic. I say the Muse likes to work crowds. Something happens when we write together that — if you trust it and go with it — can take the writing and the writer to unexpected, surprising places of memory and imagination.

In writing practice groups, we bear witness to each other's work, we learn from one another and spark each other's creativity. We share camaraderie and create community.

The Unexpected Rhythm of Different Drummers

Like tossing wildflower seeds upon a random hillside, it's difficult to determine who might flourish in the unfettered atmosphere of a writing practice group, or to define what kinds of writers would be attracted to such a gathering. Writing practice groups aren't structured for those who want critique on works in progress or for students of the craft who are looking for instruction or guidance. Rather, the writer who might benefit from participation in a community of writing practitioners is one who may not know what he wants to write, the one who is looking for his voice or style or the genre that suits the stories he has to tell. Or writers who don't know how or where to start a piece or who can't get a foothold on a story, or someone who is stuck in a piece and can't seem to find a solid path through the muck. Maybe someone who is bored, with her writing and her writing routine, or the one whose writing is so predictable he might as well just tell the reader to fill in the blanks. The lively and varied writing styles and the unconstrained and often unconventional writers who make up a practice group can wake up any snoozing muse.

Over the lifetime of a group, writers will come and go and the energy and dynamics of a group will change. This is natural. Some attend only long enough to work through the first draft of a story or get a good start on a novel, then drop away. Others try it out for a week or two, barely dip a toe in the creative waters, and decide it's not for them. More than a few come once then are never seen again, others come until they get bored or scared or feel like it's time to try something else, something with more structure now that they've got all this raw stuff to work with. Partnerships and alliances are formed, friendships are made, and on some rare and giddy occasions love happens. Not often do people go away mad, but sometimes they do. Or feelings get hurt. Writing toes get stepped on. Like any group, it's up to each participant to take to heart the meaning of community and assume individual responsibility for the well-being of the whole. Writing practice groups thrive on the infusion of new members, varied voices, and a different concoction of energy. All this is good for the writing.

Writing practice groups can be as large as a dozen or more, or as small as three or four members. I've worked with larger crowds, but more than fifteen and the whole thing can get a bit unwieldy. Not enough time for everyone to read, for one thing, and reading aloud what's just been written is an important part of the process. With larger gatherings, space might become a factor, too. And certainly opportunities for intimacy might get lost among the air pockets created by so many writers writing and reading and breathing together. Ideal size: somewhere between five and ten participants.

Writer's Phenomenon #53 says, "Requirements for organization and structure are in direct proportion to the number of people involved in a group." Which means, a group of five can operate easily with ad hoc agreement among its members, while collectives of twelve or fifteen call for more framework, which means more leadership.

⌨ Writer's Phenomenon #53

"Requirements for organization and structure are in direct proportion to the number of people involved in a group."

✍ Writing Practice Prompts

- _____ is the color I remember
- Write about being in bad company
- A chance encounter
- It was her best idea
- Write about awakening early
- Write about a slight curve

Just as there's more than one way to tell the same story, there are different constructs that will work for successful writing practice groups. Here are some suggestions.

Every Tuesday at 2:00

An ongoing, drop-in group open to anyone who wants to participate. No preregistration is necessary; no commitment is made, except to write when you do show up.

For these groups to work, there must be a regular meeting place and time. Every Tuesday from 2:00 to 3:00 P.M. in the community room of the library, for example, or 3:00 to 4:30 P.M. the first and third Saturday of each month in the back room of the Book Garden Café.

It's best for drop-in groups to meet in a public place rather than someone's home. This way privacy or security concerns are virtually nonissues. Cafés can work well if the proprietor is agreeable. And proprietors are more likely to be agreeable if everyone orders something. One of my sessions got booted out of a café, even after we'd spent more than five dollars each for lunch. We didn't clear the gathering with management ahead of time, and they didn't want us taking up the table space. Lesson: go where you're welcome and leave a big tip.

In some public places problems may arise around reading work aloud. Other customers may not want to listen to the readings and some writers might be too shy to read aloud in a public space. I've heard of places where a sort of censorship was implied because of the concern management voiced about the sensibilities of other patrons. As you look for supportive and accommodating places to hold your groups, make certain the reading portion can be both safe and out loud.

Also important for the success of drop-in groups is the commitment of certain members to serve as leaders for the day. Leaders volunteer to take responsibility for running the session, or at least making certain the space is ready when other writers show up. The leadership role can rotate, or one person can take on responsibility for a specified period of time. Appointment, election, drawing names, or volunteering — each group can determine its method.

The reticent writer hems and haws and hesitates and while everyone else is riding the wave of imagination or memory or whatever propels them forward into the sea of their story, she sits on the shore still wearing her shoes, gazing into the distant horizon. Come time for discussion, she holds back and doesn't make eye contact, offers up no comments, doesn't participate in any conversation. You might call her shy; she is probably scared. Give her time, invite her in. Be patient.

Participation can come through word of mouth, at the invitation of other members, through publicity such as posters, flyers, and notices in local newspapers, announcements at literary gatherings, Web listings, or just the happy chance of someone being in the right place at the right time. Most writers I know tend to hang out in places where they're likely to encounter their own kind, so it wouldn't be surprising to have a new member emerge from between the stacks at a bookstore, notebook in hand, and join your group.

The key to making a drop-in group work is tenacity, especially in the beginning. It takes time to build a core of committed practitioners. When I began my Brown Bag Writing Group in 1993, only two people appeared for the first meeting and one of them wasn't even a writer. Neither showed up again and for the next couple of weeks, I was the only one at the table.

Even after all these years of weekly gatherings, participation fluctuates; attendance can go from five to fifteen and back to six. One Tuesday after several years of regular meetings, there were only two of us. We wrote anyhow. Holding the space is critical, keeping the faith is encouraged, and writing no matter who shows up is fundamental.

Just among Friends — And a Few Invited Others

Another type of writing practice group is the closed group with membership made up of writers who know each other from connections literary and otherwise. Participation is usually by invitation from one of the members.

This group may meet regularly even though the meeting places might vary (a café this week, the park next week, someone's home the week after, and a train ride to the next town another time) and the time may shift. As with any group, the stability of a regular meeting time and place generally promotes participation; still it can be fun for the writers and good for the writing to create extra sessions or plan special events. One loosely knit community I was a part of arranged overnight retreats to out-of-the-way places where we surrounded ourselves with nature and gave ourselves over to the writing life for brief and inspirational interludes.

Writing Practice Prompts

- If I'd known then
- Write about falling stars
- Write about stolen moments
- Write about cheap thrills
- You're asleep. You're not at home
- Write about a disappearance

Generally, a closed group is smaller and members know each other well enough that any formal leadership or organizational structure beyond regular meeting time and place is unnecessary. Informality and spontaneity are the hallmarks.

A problem that sometimes arises is the easy slide from writing group to social group. At a break in the conversation someone looks at her watch and notices that suddenly half the meeting has been eaten up along with the scones and coffee and there's hardly time left for a serious bout of writing. One solution is for the person who has taken on the role of timekeeper for the day to note the "start writing time" and inform the group when that time has arrived.

At a Writing Practice Session

Practice groups can meet for as brief as an hour or as long as members want. Longer than three hours, however, and stamina becomes an influencing factor. My regular drop-in practice sessions go for about an hour, marathons for six or more, after which we've all morphed to the consistency of noodles. But weariness does have its blessings. When we're tired, when we think we have written all we're good for, when defenses are down and the guard has left the palace gate, we often write our most freewheeling, authentic, and daring pieces. There is a sense of letting go and a "who cares" attitude that gives access to deep recesses where imagination lives and anything can happen. But even maintaining the consistency of meeting and writing for an hour a week can have a dramatic effect on the writing and the writer. "We are what we repeatedly do," said Aristotle.

Each writing practice session will require a leader/timekeeper. For my drop-in groups I begin with a reading of the rules: "Guidelines for Writing Practice" (see page 108). This liturgical reading allows for a settling-in time. Participants get comfortable in their chairs, get all their accoutrements aligned and ready — pens, notebooks, water bottle or coffee cup. Invoking the guidelines sets the tone for our intentions and reminds us of the ways of our practice. Some use the recitation of

✐ **Writing Practice Prompts**

- Following the narrow path
- Nighttime rituals
- Write about the inherent dangers
- "The first fruit began to ripen and fall" (after Roger Aplon)
- There were rumors
- Write about leaving town

the rules as a meditation into the writing. Others think of it as a "calling of the muse."

By the time the guidelines have been read, participants are ready to write. This is when the topic is announced, and the amount of time that will be devoted to writing.

"Write about avenues of escape," the leader says. "We'll write for seventeen minutes, and I'll let you know when there are a few minutes left."

Writers fall to the task. Some stare at a middle space for a moment, then finding an image to ride, climb aboard. Others simply begin writing with no hesitation, and for the next fifteen minutes the only sound is the scratching of pen across page, an occasional sniffle or giggle or sigh as words find their way from within to without. The turning of a page, the scuffling through a bag as someone runs out of ink and searches for another pen, the jangle of bracelets.

Writing practice is almost always done by hand. Though some who work on computers would like to bring their laptops, others in the group find the irregular tap-tapping on the keyboard distracting and almost always lob grimaces of annoyance toward the typist. Computers, cell phones, beepers, pagers, music (unless it's part of the prompt), and talking toys are all discouraged. A pen with a roller ball is about as high-tech as a writing practice group wants to be.

At the fifteen-minute mark into the seventeen-minute exercise, the leader announces, "two more minutes," or "take just a few minutes to finish," and renewed intensity buzzes around the table as writers lean into their notebooks to complete the writing. Finally, "time's up" is announced and one by one, participants find a way to end.

A writing time of fifteen to twenty-two minutes works well for this kind of focused writing. Any longer and it becomes difficult to sustain the intensity — especially for those inexperienced in the process — and shorter may not allow time enough to sink to a deeper level, though I know some writers who, from the very start, are able to drop into their groove. Much depends on whether the topic evokes an immediate image

✎ Writing Practice Prompts

- It was all pretense
- This is what I want
- Write about a break-in
- Write about an ending
- "It's where the secret details are" (after Sabrina Ward Harrison)
- You were taking a nap

♀ ♀ Program for a Writing Practice Group

- Welcome and introductions

  (Usually we just go around the table for names, no lengthy introductions, especially if participants already know one another.)
- Reading of "Guidelines for Writing Practice"

  (or another opening that settles the group in and sets the intention)
- Announcement of prompt and length of writing time
- Writing
- "Time's up" announcement, preceded by a "two-minute notice"
- Reading aloud
- Second writing (if time allows), followed by readings
- Closure

  (any announcements or reminders and acknowledgment of the work done: "Thanks for coming. Keep writing.")

that's hot and whether the writer is present for the writing. Sometimes life interferes. Bad traffic or bad lunch or bad news can all derail our train of thought. Still, the tension of the timed writing will almost always override the distractions of daily life and claim surrender to the page.

The size of the group and how much total time is allowed for the meeting will determine how long each round of writing can be. If there are fifteen or more participants and only an hour for the session, the writing time will be shorter (thirteen to fifteen minutes). I've also led sessions with as little as ten-minute writes, or, with smaller groups, one round of seventeen or eighteen minutes and, after everyone has read, another "quickie" of two or three minutes. Often these short takes following a longer go-round will produce an outrageous or funny few lines or a suddenly profound paragraph.

Groups that meet for a couple of hours or more can do several rounds of writing with different lengths for each one. For example, start with five minutes, then do ten, then fifteen, then back to ten, and end with another five, allowing time to read after each writing.

These short exercises are not intended for neat beginnings, middles, and ends. There's not enough time for completed writings, though some writers are amazingly adept at creating a whole piece within any given time limit — even the short takes. Some continue writing after time's up because they can't bear to have the thing left open-ended. I have come to accept the anxiety of an unfinished work as part of the process. The piece may or may not be completed, it may be continued on the next go-round, or later at home or in some café. Maybe weeks from when it was begun. Maybe never. The point of writing practice isn't to produce a specific thing. Rather, to practice is to practice is to practice is to practice.

Giving Voice to the Writing

Make time for reading aloud after each writing exercise. This is as important as the writing. The purpose isn't for feedback or critique; the work is too raw and unfinished for that. There's no applause either, even though some of the passages may spontaneously move us to such. Rather, hearing the words out loud allows the writer to locate the knotty bone of truth in the work, if it's there, and to hear his or her writer's voice. There are other reasons for reading out loud: listening for repetition and cliché, to feel the breathing of the piece, its heartbeat. And, often, the writer won't even know what he or she has written until it's given voice.

Not everyone will want to read out loud, and no one should be required to. Sometimes what gets written is too personal to be read at group level, especially if the writer is new and hasn't developed a level of trust and intimacy that allows for such exposure and vulnerability. Or maybe a writer will feel that the piece is just too awful to be spoken. Most often this is the individual's critical judgment of herself rather than the truth. Almost every work that is written has at least one fresh phrase, one image that's worth keeping, a single word that rises like a pure and astonishing note above the circle of listeners. Gentle encouragement is sometimes all it takes for the change of a reticent mind. Or this writer may need a settling-in time and after a few sessions, she'll be, if not eager, at least willing to give voice to her writing. Fact is, the longer the hesitation to read out loud, the more difficult it becomes. Like diving headfirst into the pool or pulling off a Band-Aid in one quick yank, reading the piece aloud in spite of its perceived clunkiness or hushed intimacies may be the swiftest and best initiation. And remember, critique and feedback aren't the purpose of writing practice.

Note: Crying is allowed and not to be "fixed."

It's not unusual during communal writing for participants to go to deep and tender places that reveal past hurts and fragile secrets. Sometimes a writer will be surprised by emotion that surfaces when she reads a piece aloud. It didn't seem to be there during the writing. Writing from the quasi consciousness of intuition, without censorship or rational thought, a person may dip into a place of unexpected emotions that reach full bloom only when exposed to the sunlight of the voice. When this happens, it's best to allow the reader time to breathe into the feelings, then to continue reading. Even though it might feel

♦ ♦ Give Voice to the Writing

Reading aloud after each writing is as important as the writing itself. Some thoughts to remember:

- No critique or feedback. The writing is too raw for that. Just acknowledge the work done.
- No applause. We're not writing for approval; we're writing for practice.
- Not everyone will want to read out loud and no one should be required to.
- Let the readings occur in a spontaneous order, as writers are moved to read.
- Gentle encouragement is sometimes all it takes for a reticent writer to read.
- Crying is allowed, and not to be "fixed."
- Remember to breathe.

✎ Writing Practice Prompts

- "One night is as dark as the next" (after Lois Marie Harrod)
- Write about ordinary days
- Write about something that's broken
- "This is the story of my birth" (after Karen Swank)
- Write about something stolen
- She held it in her hand

awkward or uncomfortable, others in the group should stay present and maintain a silence, which supports the writer and honors her feelings. Nothing needs to be done or said, except perhaps a soft reminder from the leader that "it's okay" or "just breathe." Usually after a few moments the writer is able to continue reading and finish the piece, a process that often leads down the gentle path of healing. The leader's role is simply to thank the writer for trusting the group enough to read and, without further comment, invite the next person to read.

Allowing the order of reading to be free-form creates a sense of safety for participants and sustains the spontaneity of the session. Also, the unstructured following of one piece by another as synchronicities occur or themes complement or oppose one another can create a surprising flow to the reading that might never happen should a regimented going-around-the-table order be imposed. This spontaneity also allows those who might be hesitant to read an opportunity to build up sufficient courage to give voice to their writing.

Sometimes, when an especially well-written piece is read aloud, others in the group, especially newcomers, who may not know the custom of "no feedback," may jump in with comments on how good the writing is, or the effect it had on them. (Another of the reasons for no feedback, besides the rawness of the material and time constraints of brief meetings, is that the same enthusiastic response is difficult to muster for writing that is less well executed.) A gentle reminder by the facilitator of the "no critique" rule and simply asking for the next volunteer to read will get things back on track again.

An Indissoluble Time

Here's what happens in writing practice groups: First, and most important for some, the writing gets done. More than a few participants have confessed that the only time they write is in their writing practice group, which is too bad because, more than anything, it's the consistency, the daily doing of the thing, that ultimately makes for better and deeper writing and a more fulfilled writer. Second, there is the celebration of spending time in community with others doing what we love — writing. No matter what we do before or after our writing group, this is the indissoluble time that fills us up.

During any given session, we may work through a sticky place in a scene, make the happy acquaintance of a new character, release wild ambition upon the page, create something new and luminous, or write the ending to something old and laden. We may reveal secrets, unlock doors, stumble over bones, or bump against ghostly rememberings. We may learn something new or experience an emotional catharsis. Writing for revenge or healing, out of anger or sorrow, imagining or wondering or just plain old curiosity — the magical "what if..." — we do it all, and maybe we do it only in the company of others.

There is yet another striking occurrence that happens in group writing. A synchronicity that is as inexplicable as creativity and as mysterious as inspiration. Two writers use the same unusual word — doppelganger, for example — or both mention Bach and Karen Carpenter in the same piece, or write about deep-rooted trees. This seemingly coincidental happenstance of words or images is so startling it never fails to take my breath away, yet so common that those of us who are veteran group writers accept it as a predictable and delightful part of the process. I've taken to jotting these synchronistic events down: two mentions of stiletto in a writing about coming to the end of the road, a couple of notes on dead presidents in a piece about what was found in a pocket, three references to secrets during a prompt taken from the first line of Margaret Atwood's *The Blind Assassin* ("All she had was a single photograph."). Long ago, before writing in groups, before making that intimate and intuitive connection I have come to expect in such gatherings, I used to call such occurrences simple coincidence, but no longer. I know there is magic afoot.

To be sure, there is still the hard and solitary work of rewriting, editing, polishing that each writer must go and do alone. But the creation stuff, the community and support and Wild Mouse ride of first draft writing — these are what a writing practice group can nurture.

♦ ♦ The Benefits of Writing Practice

- Builds self-confidence
- Enhances creativity
- Strengthens writerly self-esteem
- Produces fresh material
- Offers opportunities for exploration
- Supports risk taking
- Auditions ideas
- Provides casting couch for characters
- Expands vocabulary
- Fosters creation of writer's unique language
- Gives voice lessons
- Sets a place for the muse
- Honors commitment
- Develops trust (in yourself and your writing)
- Allows discovery of what matters
- Helps you find your voice
- Encourages spontaneity
- Invokes imagination
- Banishes fears
- Nurtures courage
- Evokes self-expression
- Sustains spirit

A Brief History of the Brown Bag Writing Group

First came the place: The Writing Center, a gathering place for writers in a renovated old building that nudged against the heart of San Diego's Gaslamp Quarter. Then the idea took form: A fifty-minute, drop-in writing practice session held every Tuesday from 12:10 to 1 P.M. We'd call it the Brown Bag Writing Group, and anybody could join. No need to pre-register, just show up. We'd keep the costs low, (only $5 when we started, in 1993, and only $5 today, nearly a decade later) and the energy high. We'd write together, working from a prompt, in writing practice sessions, and after the writing, everyone would have a chance to read aloud what he or she had written. Keep it simple, make it easy, create a safe and nurturing environment: no critique, no applause, no pressure, no expectations. Just writers writing.

While it wasn't an instant success, it didn't take long for word to get out and a few curious writers started drifting in. There were some lonely weeks in the beginning, me with one or two others, or some weeks just me, surrounded by empty tables and chairs. But by early spring, Brown Bag had become the Tuesday lunch spot for all manner of writers who wanted to chew on their words instead of a Big Mac and fries. (No eating during the sessions, only writing and reading.) Our numbers fluctuated then as they do today, eight or ten, sometimes up to fifteen or more. Nearly every week you could count on certain writers showing up and taking their same place at the table, with their same notebook and favorite pen. (No laptops allowed; the tap-tapping of the keyboard proved too distracting for the other writers.) As time passed, nearly every Tuesday you could expect a new writer to stop in and give it a try, or someone who hadn't been for a while to drop by. There is a fine, welcoming feeling of community at the gatherings.

Over the years, we've changed locations a few times. Now we meet at The Writers' Room, above a furniture consignment store in another old building. We still use some of the same tables and chairs from our first location. Some of us are still writing in our familiar brand of notebooks with the same well-grooved make of pen. But the prompts are always fresh: between four and five hundred of them, gathered in a shaggy old red notebook, with a new one added every week.

There have been newspaper stories written about us and pictures taken. Some of us have been on the radio and in videos. We celebrated our fifth anniversary with an anthology of our work and a held a reading in the park. Over the years, we've experienced the occasional flirtation or love affair among the membership, and two or three Brown Bagettes have been born. Couples come and write together. Mothers bring their daughters and writers bring out-of-town guests. Friends tote friends, "See, this is what I've been telling you about." We get notes and e-mails from those who have moved away, "I really miss Brown Bag." Our group has spawned other such gatherings and we've been replicated in a few locations across the country, even in London last I heard.

We come for the writing and for the community. You can have either one without the other, but bring them together and some kind of alchemy takes place and we, and our writing, are so much the better for it.

✐ Writing Practice Prompts

- Write about a complication
- "She dresses in . . ."
- Write about being moonstruck
- If everything is true
- Write what happened one day
- You left something behind

Write About a Day Moon:
Prompts for the Writing Practice Group

Writing prompts are created to help writers get a start on an exercise. In classes or workshops or in writing books, prompts are intended to guide the writer to work within a certain area, or to accomplish a specific task. For example, an exercise might set up a situation. Your character is tied down to the railroad tracks, the train is coming. Then you're directed to create three scenarios for what happens next. Or you might be told, Write a dialogue scene in which two characters discover a secret about each other. Or, Describe a moonlit scene as observed by four different characters: a bank robber, a teenage girl in love, a lost child, a werewolf.

Prompts created for writing practice don't give such explicit direction. They are not intended to help the writer learn some particular skill or work in a certain area. Instead, based on the idea that what each person wants to write about will emerge organically as the writing occurs, the prompts are general and wide open with the unadorned invitation to "write about..." and without additional directives such as "describe" or "create" or "remember" or "imagine."

To practice is to trust the pen and the process and to allow to appear what will. Instead of trying to think and assess and formulate using the cognitive side of the brain, writing practice simply says "Write." The intuitive is invited to spill forth images and words, rememberings and imaginings in the connect-the-dots language it speaks. In practice, you can't be sure what will emerge until you complete the session. What a surprise to find bits and pieces of an essay or scatterings of story seedlings, the bright wing of a memoir. Characters might show up to have their say. If you're lucky, a poem might grace your page. Or drawn out on the pale blue lines of your notebook paper, a series of images as rich and detailed as a Moroccan rug. The prompt itself may not have much, if anything, to do with what finally gets written. It serves only as a starting point, a place for the writer to swoop off the cliff and glide onto the winds of her imagination. "Creating is not remembering but experiencing," said Gertrude Stein. "It is the immediate feelings arranged in words as they occur to me."

A writing practice prompt might be, "Write about a full moon." One writer might describe the moon she saw from aboard a cruise ship last summer. Someone else may write a childhood memory of his grandfather that doesn't even mention the moon ("Oh, I never got to the part about the moon," he might say after the exercise). Another could create a horror story about werewolves, while the next might start an essay on the effects of the full moon on gardening.

Writing prompts can be in the form of a simple word (mosaic, moonflower, iridescent, potpourri) or the suggestion to "Write about..." (someone who left, a river, falling), a line from a poem ("A year after your death..." Czeslaw Milosz), or from a book ("She learned to tell time with her skin," from *Prodigal Summer* by Barbara Kingsolver). Anything that causes some slight hum of response as you read it can be the origin of a prompt. (Be careful not to use something too familiar or all that will appear may be the remainder of the poem or

✐ Writing Practice Prompts

- Another view
- "A midnight conversation" (after Emily Dickinson)
- It was stone fruit season
- Write about falling
- Write about being spellbound

story from the book.) On occasion I invite participants in my group to open the dictionary to a word, any word, and offer it to the next person as her prompt, and so on, around the room with each writer receiving a different word to write from. And I never read anything without a notebook by my side or sticky notes within reach. You never know when the perfect prompt will appear. ("It was a summer of blue-black nights" — Don Delillo, *Underworld;* "...fierce surprises" — a phrase from Raymond Carver; "Everybody loves the sound of a train in the distance/Everybody thinks it's true" — a song by Paul Simon; "The mixture should be highly seasoned" — directions from a cookbook.)

The real world can also be a source for writing prompts. I jot down phrases I hear during the day (a writer always eavesdrops), or something I've seen scrawled on a building ("This Is the Last Time"), or notes from a menu at lunch (juice from the ripest berries). Always, always writing practitioners have a notebook at the ready. Even directions on a cereal box have served as a writing prompt for my drop-in group ("Slide finger under flap and loosen gently"). Faulkner said there's a bit of the scavenger in every writer. This is what we do when we're collecting inspiration.

The ingredients for a good prompt are much like the ingredients of a fine meal. When they are placed before us, we let go an involuntary "ummmmm" and we feel a delightful urge to pick up the pen and dive in.

Of course, what might be rich for one person could be dry as uncooked oatmeal to another. While I wrote four furious pages on the word "hair," my friend Camille couldn't find a strand to grasp hold of. (She who has a great curly head of dark hair, soft as a baby's toy.) I like dangerous words like scar or shadow, mouth or closet. Or words that carry emotional weight such as loneliness, longing, ache, sorrow. Or rage, distrust, betrayal, scorn. And, though any writer can go anywhere with any topic, words that are too light and airy or don't have room for some kind of drama don't offer as much of a toehold as those that carry more tension. Though they might be great topics for journal writing, such words as happiness, admiration, gratitude, and cheerful are hard to sink a literary incisor into. In her book *Poemcrazy,* poet Susan

✐ Writing Practice Prompts

- This is what I cannot throw away
- Rising from sleep
- Write what you want but cannot have
- Write about a scent
- Write about being interrupted
- "It all started when ..."

Wooldridge calls certain words "loaded," ones that she says "form the outer layer of a well of associations." Look for words that cause you to lift an eyebrow or that ruffle the hair on the back of your neck. I always know I've hit upon a good topic when a murmuring of thoughtful "hmmmmms" rises from those gathered around the table.

Prompts aren't meant to be taken literally and they aren't themes for compositions or essays. Even though they give a focus, the writing isn't supposed to be just about the prompt. In fact, the writing isn't supposed to be about anything except what it wants to be. So a writer doesn't have to stay on topic to do it right. Anyway it's done is right.

Perfume Bottles and Darning Needles

Props are three-dimensional forms of prompts. For writing props, use items you can hold in your hand, or look at, or smell or touch or listen to. In a basket of props balanced on a low shelf in my bookcase are a plastic yo-yo, a kitchen whisk, a blue wooden egg, a golf tee, a pine cone, a tarnished brass napkin ring, a map of Père-Lachaise Cemetery, a strip of bark from a eucalyptus tree, a hazelnut, a Clinton/Gore sticker, a "no-sew" turkey lacer, a bottle of tincture of iodine, a tea bag (chamomile), a green plastic fountain pen, and a packet of marigold seeds. Participants at a recent marathon found twenty-five books spread out on a table, each with something tucked within its pages — a door key, a love note, a receipt from a motel, ticket stubs from the theater, a pressed violet. They were to write about the book, then write about what they found inside. Other props have included pieces of jewelry, decorative boxes (also with something placed inside), rocks and shells, bits of bones and feathers, bird nests, seeds and acorns, small toys, fruits and vegetables (the more distinct and odd the shape or color, the better), maps of cities and maps of the universe. Participants have been invited to bring love tokens, mementos from journeys, icons or other meaningful items from their own collections. These we have used as writing props.

Music can also serve the muse. I've made up special collections for specific writing practice workshops (night music for "Hot Nights, Wild

Women," or sexy music for an erotic writing workshop), and I've used music as background to write to: instrumentals (lyrics can be distracting), mostly jazz or classical or New Age. Sometimes just percussion or nature sounds recorded with music. Thunderstorms, the ocean, night sounds, crickets and songbirds. Spoken-word recordings have also been evocative.

Used book stores and thrift shops are great places to pick up old books of photographs that can be cut up and shuffled out onto a table for a writing session. I've separated mine into people and landscapes, though a mixture of the two (put this character in that landscape) can offer an interesting juxtaposition. A collection of postcards can also serve as props for a practice session. Writers are invited to use either side: the picture or the personal message. Slides projected onto a screen or blank wall, either a single photograph or a changing series, serve as bigger-than-life images from which to write.

Sometimes the spontaneous can find its way into your practice session with prompts or props that you never would have dreamed up. Once, when we were still at the old Writing Center downtown in San Diego's Gaslamp Quarter, gunshots followed fast by sirens made for a lively practice session, as did performances at the Fritz Theater, with which we shared a brick wall. And, at the eighth annual summer writing marathon at The Writers' Room, a passing parade of gay rights activists with their chants and shouts and drums beat its way into our notebooks. So if you and your group are in a public place — at a café or somewhere outside — use what's there as fodder for the writing. The art on the wall, the people passing by, the couple negotiating a date at the next table, the clouds in the sky. Everything that is, is ours for the writing.

I keep a file folder for writing prompts. It's fat as a puppy with ragged pages from my notebooks, scrambled bits of scratch pads and napkins, and sticky notes that flap like flags on a halyard when I open the drawer where they're squeezed in. I also keep a section of my notebook for prompts, and envelopes and boxes and baskets and jars full of words or sentence stems or cut apart poems, snippets of dialogue or dream images.

Use the following exercises to begin your Prompts and Props collection.

- Create a prompt that is a line from a poem.
- Use a line of dialogue for a prompt.
- Write words onto small, folded pieces of paper that you stick in an envelope to draw out for random practice sessions. Make at least two dozen.
- Copy phrases from the current book you're reading.
- While out in the world notice a sign or some graffiti or a billboard that you can use for prompts.
- In a five-minute expedition around the house, gather up a bag full of props.
- Go on a hunting and gathering junket in your neighborhood or at the local mall and bring back "found" items.
- Ask your friends to send postcards from any port of call.

Once you begin to take notice, you'll see and hear prompts everywhere. In fact, with your prompt consciousness raised, you may even find it difficult to have a conversation without stopping to write down a potential prompt, and what used to be a simple trip to the market can turn into a prop-laden hunting and gathering expedition.

Guidelines for Writing Practice

1. Keep writing. Don't stop to edit, to rephrase, to think. Don't go back and read what you've written. Each time you stop, you move out of the place of intuitive trusting to a cerebral place of judging, evaluating, comparing. If you keep your writing hand moving, you'll bypass the censor, the editor, the critic, and if you're lucky, maybe even the ego.

2. Trust your pen. Go with the first image that appears. "First thought, best thought" reminds us that the first image comes from your intuitive mind, where the creative process finds its foothold. The pen is the tool of the intuitive. It won't take you further or deeper than you want to go, but it might take you to uncharted places you never thought about consciously.

3. Don't judge your writing. Don't compare, analyze, criticize. Remember that what gets written in writing practice is the roughest of rough drafts — writing that is pouring directly from intuition, too fragile and raw for judgments. Remember to be your own best friend — nonjudgmental, accepting, tolerant, loving, kind, and patient. And remember to laugh sometimes. At yourself and your writing.

4. Let your writing find its own form. Form will come organically out of what you write. You don't have to have a beginning, a middle, and an end for what you write in practice sessions. Nor does it have to fit into some container labeled story or essay or poem. If you try to force form, you may miss

---

Even in a group, this one is alone. Maybe you feel like he never really lets you in, or that you don't really know him. The loner doesn't mean offense; it's just his way. Singular. Solitary. A bit withdrawn and maybe even mysterious. Sometimes being a loner is a defense; but the true loner is one who likes it that way. Don't take it personally. Allow him his distance.

revelations that might otherwise appear, and letting go of any preconceived ideas of what you want to write will set free a tremendous energy to write what wants to be written.

5. Don't worry about the rules. It doesn't matter if your grammar is incorrect, your spelling wrong, your syntax garbled, or your punctuation off. Not during practice sessions anyhow. Worrying about these rules during writing practice can trip up the intuitive flow of words and images. The time to edit, correct, and polish is during rewrites, not during practice.

6. Let go of any expectations. Expectations set you up so you're always ahead of yourself rather than being present in the moment. This is why it's good to dive right into the writing topic with no time to think of what you'll write or how best to shape your writing around a subject. Before you begin writing, clear your mind, settle into place, breathe, and simply begin. Let your writing surprise you.

7. Kiss your frogs. First-draft writing doesn't have to be good, it won't always be good, and even when it is good, among the good will be some not so good. Remember, this is just practice. You write what you write. Every writer experiences bad days and sloppy, swampy writing. This is the frog-kissing phenomenon of creative writing. Sometimes you get the handsome prince and sometimes you get the frog. The point is, no matter what, you show up at the pond.

8. Tell the truth. Every time you write you have an opportunity to tell the truth. And sometimes it's only through writing that you can know the truth. Be willing to go to the scary places that make your hand tremble and your handwriting get a little out of control. Be willing to tell your secrets. It's risky, but if you don't write the truth, you chance writing that is glib, shallow, or bland. Go to the edge of what feels safe and step off. The net will appear.

9. Write specific details. Your writing doesn't have to be

Guidelines for Writing Practice

1. Keep writing
2. Trust your pen
3. Don't judge your writing
4. Let your writing find its own form
5. Don't worry about the rules
6. Let go of any expectations
7. Kiss your frogs
8. Tell the truth
9. Write specific details
10. Write what matters
11. Read your writing aloud
12. Date your page and write the topic at the top

†

The ambitious writer doesn't hide her short stories in a drawer when she completes them, she sends them out. She starts with The New Yorker *and works her way down. She doesn't hesitate to approach a successful writer and ask questions, or follow an agent into the elevator so she can give a pitch. Even if she's shaking in her Hush Puppies, she goes after what she wants. Being in the right place at the right time, knowing the right people, getting lucky, a chance encounter, a fortunate happenstance — all these might play a role in getting what you always dreamed of, but the ambitious writer is the one with energy and fortitude and a stick-to-itiveness that the Elmer's folks would like to patent.*

factual, but the specificity of detail brings it alive. It does not matter if the tree you sat beneath was a sycamore or a eucalyptus, but naming it one or the other will paint a clearer picture. The truth isn't in the facts; it's in the detail, and details, truthfully rendered, bring your writing to life and create connection points for the reader. Pay attention, notice what you notice — especially through your five senses — and write it down.

10. Write what matters. If you don't care about what you're writing, neither will your readers. Write about what interests you, what bothers you, what you don't understand, what you want to learn more about. There's not enough time to write what doesn't matter to you, and only you can say what's important. Write with passion.

11. Read your writing aloud after you've completed your practice session. You'll find out what you've written, what you care about, and when the writing is "working." Reading aloud lets you know when the writing is repetitious or trite. You pick up clichés and sense obstacles that might get in the way of the reader. Reading aloud tells you when you're writing with authenticity and when you've found your writer's voice.

12. Date your page and write the topic at the top. This will keep you grounded in the present and help you reference pieces you might want to use in something else. A review of the dates in your practice notebook can provide insights about your writing self: the rhythm of your writing, cycles of ease and creativity and cycles of hard going and dead ends, the intricate weave of associations and connections and which types of prompts are most evocative for you. This is all fodder for our hungry minds.

The "Guidelines for Writing Practice" originally appeared in *A Writer's Book of Days*. They have been adapted here.

Profile: Thursday Writers Group

On any given Thursday except Thanksgiving, Thursday Writers gathers for its weekly session of writing practice. The group has been together for more than seven years, has seen its ranks swell upward of twenty and shrivel down to five or six and has moved meeting locations four times.

Designed to accommodate the after-work writing practitioner, Thursday Writers meets from 5:40 to 6:30 P.M. If traffic is especially tangled on the I-5 or I-8, you can expect a smaller group, or many late arrivals, some who tiptoe in, sneak a look at the top line of the leader's notebook for the topic and plop down in any available chair to begin their writing. Thursday Writers is a drop-in writing practice group I started, following upon the success of the Brown Bag Writing Group that meets every Tuesday at noon. I have to admit that at least part of the reason for beginning another group had to do with my own joyful and productive experience of writing in community. Our longevity may owe something to our early roots with The Writing Center, but even more than that, it has to do with our stability. Because even though we've changed locations four times, we've maintained the same format and meeting time. (A mailing list of participants with occasional post-card notices keeps everyone informed of changes.) The primary factor in the group's staying power, I believe, is the commitment to commu-nity of the writers who participate.

Currently the group meets in The Writers' Room, a gathering place for writers situated above a furniture consignment store in the University Heights area of San Diego. A scattering of tables and chairs in a quiet room creates an easy ambiance, free parking and cafés close by make it especially writer friendly. A five-dollar fee, which is collected in an enve-lope that is passed around along with a sign-in sheet, goes to pay for rental of the room, the occasional mailings, and a gratuity for the leader.

Though some of us have studied writing formally, we're like thou-sands of other writers who earn their living otherwise. We fit the writ-ing in the odd morning hours before the sun and our families arise or long, long into the night after everything else is done and the only thing left is the writing. And always, the writing practice.

✐ Writing Practice Prompts

- Write about giving in
- Someone gives you a message
- Write about a front porch
- This is the taste of what had been lost
- Write about a danger-ous intersection
- "I linger with an ache always" (after Juan Felipe Herrera)

Some of us are published — a story here, a poem there, a book, an article, an essay. One of our ranks is a successful songwriter. Among us, some are writing novels, some short fiction, others essays and poetry. And some are still looking for the form that will carry the voice, winged and true, to a place that feels like home.

A few of us write for a living — we call ourselves commercial writers: marketing, advertising, public relations, technical writing. Writing for money, not for love. Not the same. And whatever we do for a living outside the group, it doesn't matter. The place that we connect, our touch point, is the writing.

Age doesn't matter either; we span the years — early twenties to nearing sixty. On any given day, with a blank piece of paper, a pen and time, anything can happen for any of us.

By now most of the regulars know the "rules," a set of guidelines that are read before each writing session. We adapted ours from Natalie Goldberg's book *Wild Mind,* loosely altering and changing them over the years to create our own, which currently number eleven. "Keep your hand moving," the rules begin. "Don't worry about spelling, punctuation, or grammar." "Go for the jugular." "You're free to write the worst junk in America." We added our last rule, number eleven — "Remember to breathe" — at a meeting a few summers ago when the air lumbered with humidity and for some reason tension in the room was palpable. Sometimes we turn the words around and read, "Breathe to remember."

Like most practice sessions, the wording of the prompt itself doesn't really matter, what wants to be written will emerge beneath each writer's pen. Still, those of us who've been writing together for awhile have come to know and anticipate returning characters or the particular and familiar practice voice of certain writers among us. Whether the topic is "Write about an interlude," "You've come to the end of the road," or "She was wearing a disguise," Warren might write about the girl in the second story window, or the old and alcoholic woman who lived in the apartment across the hall, or, more recently, grandparents yet to immigrate from Russia. Susan will most certainly write another

✐ Writing Practice Prompts

- Someone said,
- "This is not what you expected" (after Lizzie Wann)
- Write about coming home
- Write about rainlight
- I remember smelling
- Write what is alive in winter
- Two or three things I know about

charming piece featuring the "duckbutts," tiny people who wear costumes and do magic and are seen only by Sylvia. Brillianta, a one-legged transvestite of grandiose manner and dramatic costumes might appear on Steve's page. Either this or a touching personal narrative essay that evokes a "holy silence" after it's read. Karen may write prose or a poem. Whichever, you can be certain the language will be lyrical and the implications sensual.

Meanwhile, Michelle will add another scene to her novel featuring Epiphany Rose, a character who appeared out of nowhere one Thursday a few years ago. Dave will take us on a whimsical language journey of his lively imagination; David might write a profound and moving piece with imagery and symbology abounding or a hilarious short short with quirky characters set in an English garden. "More tea, dear?" All the while, Joe writes furiously, his yellow notebook pages creating a breeze across the table as he flips one after the other in his urgency to get down an edgy piece of fiction that satirizes certain famous writers or any suspect cultural milieu; his wit is nothing if not wide-ranging and unflinching. You can expect blood. My own writing may speak with the voice of one of the characters from my novel or turn into a meandering half memory that almost always reveals itself to have a shadowy footprint in another place and time.

Not everyone reads each time. A closed notebook with pen resting atop is the unspoken signal that whatever was written won't be given voice this Thursday. Maybe next time. Or the time after. There will always be another Thursday. Another gathering of the Thursday Writers. "Until then," we say, "keep writing."

6 WRITING WORKSHOP GROUPS

Defining the Term

Like so many other American words, the term workshop, as it relates to a creative writing workshop, has come to be both noun and verb. Following are my own definitions.

Workshop (*n*) A group session in which creative works are developed; an experiential class or seminar in which participants create new work or continue works in progress.

Workshop (*v*) To review a piece of creative work with other writers; for example, "Has your manuscript been workshopped yet?" or "That poem has had the life workshopped right out of it."

In academic settings, MFA programs, and at some writers conferences, a workshop generally means a read and critique session in which members of the group review participants' manuscripts.

For our purposes, we use the term "workshop group" to mean a group that comes together in the more traditional sense of the word — to interact and exchange information as it relates to their writing.

Again, what's the difference between a read and critique group, a writing practice group and a workshop group? In a read and critique, participants critique material written outside the group. In writing practice, a prompt is given and writers go to it without any further direction, spontaneously getting on the page whatever comes. There is no critique or feedback after the writing is completed. In a writing workshop, participants create new material based on some aspect of the craft or they work on particular projects, usually with specific guidelines or instruction or under the direction of a facilitator. In workshop groups, the principles of writing practice may be used in the creation of new material and, when writers have had a chance to edit and rewrite their material, read and critique might be part of a session. More information follows on how these elements are included in the work of a workshop. But for now, let it be said that for those who want to stretch their writing muscles, give new techniques a spin, learn how to and why to and when to, few gatherings can be more invigorating than a writing workshop.

Show, Don't Tell

Picture a warm Saturday afternoon, a comfortable room with tables and chairs, seven or eight writers around a table, the requisite latte cups and water bottles, notebooks open, pens ready. Here we have a just-beginning writer who wants to write a novel, a novelist who's working on going beyond the bare bones of her plot, a short-story writer who can't seem to complete any of his stories, an eager journaler who's ready to move into fiction and a few others. They've come together to learn aspects of how to "show, don't tell" in a half-day workshop.

After the welcome and introductions, the workshop leader might begin the workshop in a brief discussion about using description to set the emotional mood of a place, maybe telling the group that emotional description can be conveyed through colors, sounds, smells, or any of the sense words, through images, and the use of metaphor or simile. Then she reads an example from a published work.

After she finishes, she may ask participants what emotions they experienced during the reading, and perhaps read another paragraph from another writer that creates a different mood.

Then she gives an exercise: "Write a paragraph describing a room you love to be in, then, in another paragraph, describe a place where you are afraid." For the next ten minutes, the participants work in their own notebooks. After they've completed the exercise, there will be an opportunity for some to read their work aloud.

"For those who want to stretch their writing muscles, give new techniques a spin, learn how to and why to and when to, few gatherings can be more invigorating than a writing workshop."

At the end of three or four hours of such exercises, they may be weary but probably feel pretty good about the work they've done. Another investment of time and maybe a little bit of money spent learning the craft and honoring themselves as writers. To be sure, they could have done the same work at home alone. There's no shortage of writing books that give good advice and offer up great exercises.

But coming together to do the work in group, these writers have the advantage of learning not only from their own work, but from the work of the other writers as well. And to get feedback on what they've produced. In all the years I've done exercises from writing books on my bookshelves, and there have been dozens (of years and exercises), I've never felt like I was part of something larger than myself. Or felt like my efforts were taken seriously by others. Or laughed out loud. (Loud and sometimes raucous laughter is one of the signs of a good workshop.) And I never got any feedback, either. Left to my own inexperienced eye, I didn't know if I'd done the thing right or missed the mark completely. There was the exercise, left dangling in my notebook.

To be sure, I did learn some things reading all those books and working through the exercises, and some of the suggestions did help me blaze a trail through a thicket of my own inexperience, and occasionally, something bright would spark off my willingness and blundering through. More often than not, though, I found myself attaching sticky notes to certain pages with the intention of returning to the exercise "when I had more time" or "when I need it."

A writing workshop implies that the writer will be creating new work on the spot generated from exercises suggested by the workshop leader. Whether it's a two-hour workshop at a writers conference, a daylong session presented by another writer, a weekend intensive at a retreat center, or a two-week experience in another country, when an event is billed as a writing workshop, bring your notebook and pens or your laptop and be ready to work. Take notes. Ask questions. Let go of any self-consciousness and go for it. The best way to learn is by doing. Make mistakes. "Try again. Fail better," playwright and novelist Samuel Beckett advised.

We'll get around to this one later. Just kidding. But you see, that's how the procrastinator is. As soon as, when I have more time, after, in a few (minutes, hours, days, weeks, months, ad infinitum). Procrastination comes from fear. It comes from lack of commitment or passion, or from not believing in yourself or your work. Maybe the procrastinator suffers from just plain laziness or lack of interest, or at the other end of that road, from perfectionism or the need to write something Important or Profound. At the read and critique session, the procrastinator didn't bring new pages to the sessions because he didn't get around to writing them. Or the pages he did bring are in pretty rough shape because they were written an hour before the group met. If you've got a procrastinator in your group, you can help by not accepting the explanations no matter how reasonable they sound, by pulling the procrastinator's covers, by gently confronting every excuse with the reality of what you're hearing. In my experience as a teacher and member of dozens of writing groups, of all the reasons writers don't write, procrastination based on fear is the most prevalent.

✝
For some, writing is like a series of love affairs. The initial attraction, the mad infatuation, the falling, falling, falling in love, it's so hot it consumes the writer; all he can do is think about it, work on it, be with it. Then, something changes: the thing gets a little difficult, starts to make demands, have expectations, and the thrill is gone. It wasn't The One after all, just another promise gone to bones. There are many reasons a writer might not finish a project; most have to do with fear. Fear of failure, fear of success, fear the idea wasn't all that great to start with, fear there might not be another idea, fear of discovering he's not a writer after all, fear of discovering he really is. Those who share a writers group with this dilettante might encourage him to see a project through to the end, no matter what. Not finishing can be habit forming, and it's not a habit that serves a writer well.

A workshop is also a great place to meet other writers, especially those who are working within the same genre or area of interest. Poets attend poetry workshops; you will meet fiction writers at workshops on characterization or plot, and memoirists at a session on writing your life story.

Some workshops may be billed as "beginners" or "advanced." Sometimes you may be requested to submit material for acceptance into the workshop, along with a small reading fee. Workshop fees themselves can range from just a few dollars to the price of the down payment on a new car. Cost isn't necessarily a good criterion to measure the value of the workshop. I've gone to workshops priced under fifty dollars and filled a notebook with valuable stuff that I continued to use long after the event was over. And, once I paid a few hundred dollars to hear a writer I truly admired talk about his failed love life. How he got to that instead of the material we were supposed to work on, I can't say. Maybe I'd never attend another of his workshops, but I still buy his books, and I confess it was embarrassingly thrilling to hear those intimate details.

But do you need an instructor? Absolutely not! In his book *Writing without Teachers*, Peter Elbow writes that the teacherless writing class is a place where there is learning, but not teaching. "It is possible to learn something and not be taught. It is possible to be a student and not have a teacher," he writes. Creating a writing workshop group of peers can be a great way to learn the craft, share community, and expand your writing experience and knowledge.

Say you're in a read and critique group and members decide they'd like to work on a particular element of the craft. Learning more about dialogue, for example, or how to write scenes. A special workshop session can be structured with different members volunteering to bring in exercises from writing books, or lead an exercise they've done in a class or workshop.

Or maybe a writing practice group wants to focus on sessions in which members create material on a specific topic or around a theme, which will then be edited and produced in a chapbook or presented at a reading. For example, our Brown Bag and Thursday Writers groups have staged readings for our anniversary celebrations and, to mark our fifth year, we created an anthology of our work. Instead of your regular writing practice meetings, or in addition to them, your group could hold a series of workshop sessions.

The next section offers guidelines and suggestions for creating your own writing workshop groups, and staging writing workshops. Have at it!

Building a Workshop Group

Though there are those who vote for diversity under any circumstances, generally a workshop group will better serve its participants if everyone is toiling in the same literary field, or at least genres where workshop topics can cross-fertilize. A workshop for poets on creating haiku probably won't be of much interest to those who want to work on screenplays; creating fiction from real life might not help writers who want to freelance articles for trade or mass market magazines.

"Believe me, there's solitude aplenty out there, and whatever illusion of community can be created by the honorable fabrication of a workshop, well, that's fine by me."

— Geoffrey Wolff

On the other hand, workshops on how to create interesting characters or write dialogue or the nuances of "show, don't tell" can be useful for those working in fiction, creative nonfiction, personal narrative, and memoir, even playwriting and screenplay writing.

Like writing practice groups, workshop groups can be structured in a couple of different ways.

1. Keep the group to the participating members.

Restricting the group to participating members will help maintain the focus and continuity and determine how the time will be spent, what topics will be covered, and who will take leadership.

An ongoing workshop group that meets regularly will have the benefit of the camaraderie and support that come with participants knowing one another. Familiarity has its comforts. You know that Steve is always going to laugh at your best lines and that Allison is often moved to tears. You know to expect some fine turns of phrases from Suzanne and that Amy will be amazingly complete in whatever she writes and that Anitra will offer up something fresh and smart. When Marcy makes her sharp comments, you don't take them personally anymore. That's just her way. You can always learn from these writers.

There's a sense of community, too. Everyone wants good writing for everyone else. Competition and comparisons that sometimes show up when you're new to a group fall by the wayside of mutual support as you work together.

Like writing practice groups and read and critique groups, these workshop groups have a regular meeting time and place and hold to them. Format is already determined and group members slip into the familiar routine — and often the same, familiar seats — with little pre-amble. Everyone can get right to work.

2. Open the group to anyone who wants to participate.

If your group is small, or if you want to offer opportunities for par-ticipation by other writers in the community, you may want to make yours an open group. Though the program may be set by the core mem-bership or a program committee, anyone and everyone is invited to attend the sessions. You can determine a "season" or series of work-shops in advance, then provide information to the public at large. Maybe your group develops a mailing list or an e-mail list of interested writers. Use all the normal methods of getting the word out: flyers, list-ings in local publications, on Web pages, word of mouth.

In this case, you may want to charge a fee to cover materials and mailing costs, space rental, and refreshments.

Many writers who otherwise might be as allergic to the classroom as they are to chalk dust like to present workshops for other writers. Also writers who teach at local colleges or universities might appreciate the casual interaction and camaraderie of a few hours with a tribe of local writers who are committed to the craft and passionate about their work. After toiling away a semester with pre-law students or math majors who have to take Comp 101 as part of their undergrad require-ments, a writing workshop could be a stimulating proposition. If you've got a solid group of workshoppers looking for a teacher to lead a special session, don't be afraid to ask. Offer a fee and make all the arrangements, including getting a healthy turnout, so all the instructor has to do is show up. Tell him to bring copies of his books along if he has them. Maybe he can make a few sales, too.

What Workshop Works?

Want to learn more about the elements of the craft? Feel unsure of the genre that fits you best? Haven't tried enough of the different styles to know what fits best and think maybe exploring a variety of genres would suit your needs? Don't even know what styles are or what genre means, just want to make noise on paper? You and a group of writer friends have in mind a performance piece you'd like to create? A chapbook you want to produce? Or a text you want to work through together?

Answering these questions might help you get a better handle on the type of workshop that would suit your group best. The "Wants, Needs, and Intentions" checklist on page 21 may help. If you want to focus on the craft, have group members suggest specific aspects they'd like to work on. For example, characterization, dialogue, writing scenes, plotting, style, voice, dramatic structure, et cetera.

Want to experiment with different genres? Use the same method. Members choose subjects such as "short stories," "free verse poetry," "flash fiction," "memoir," "monologue," and so forth. Volunteers lead sessions on a particular topic. Writing books (there are hundreds and later in this chapter I've named some I've worked with; others are listed in the Bibliography), Web sites, and magazines such as *Writer's Digest* offer instruction and exercises that can be used to structure a workshop around.

Following this section are detailed descriptions and guidelines for four different types of workshops, and on pages 134 to 135, suggested workshop topics.

How Many?

One of the criteria that identifies *workshop* is the size of the group. Generally these gatherings are kept small — five to fifteen people. For

Not certain what type of workshop best suites your needs? Try a five- to seven-minute freewriting on what you want to learn more about in your writing. Don't think. Just write. Let your inner-writer reveal his or her desires.

good reason, too. Workshop implies an exchange of ideas and a good measure of hands-on, experiential writing. The term itself suggests intimacy, although once I attended a workshop in Southern California with somewhere upward of eight hundred other participants. The organizers split us into several groups so we weren't all in one session at one time. Still, it wasn't what you'd call intimate with more than two hundred of us chanting "Ode to the West Wind" along with Allen Ginsberg. It was a lively experience though. You should have heard us!

So what's a good number for a workshop? A group of twenty participants, let alone two hundred, becomes unwieldy, especially if you're working without a net — that is with peer leadership rather than an experienced workshop facilitator. On the other end, only three or four people and it becomes difficult to keep energy revved. A size that works well is more than five and under a dozen. You'll want to have time for lots of interaction and discussion and space around the writing exercises.

How Often?

The type of group as well as its size and the objectives will answer the "how often to meet" question. I've participated in workshops where members rotate leadership/programming responsibilities and they've been able to hold a steady pace of weekly meetings. Others like to have some breathing space around their meetings, especially if preparing the program takes a lot of time. Maybe they meet only monthly.

Workshop groups that build their sessions around a particular text may work best with a weekly commitment over the course of time it takes to work through the book. Twelve weeks in the case of Julia Cameron's book *The Artist's Way,* and fifty-two using Robert Ray's *Weekend Novelist.* On the other hand, because it's structured in months as well as days, groups using my book *A Writer's Book of Days* may meet only once each month. (Even though it is a "book of days," daily is difficult enough for one writer, but a bit much for any two writers, let alone a group.)

Special project workshop groups generally have a deadline for their project, which becomes the determining factor of how often they meet. The Second Story Writers, a women's writing ensemble I participated

Can't wait to finish his novel, talks in terms of weeks and months instead of years like the rest of us. So anxious to complete the scene he skipped everything but the dialogue. Never mind about those rewrites, he's going to just barrel through to the end even if some of the suggested changes are going to leave holes the size of a suburban bungalow in his story. This writer hasn't figured out that it isn't the product that we should be concerned with; it's the process. No matter how many novels we finish or stories we write or poems we craft, there will always be something more to write. We never finish.

in, met every few weeks at the beginning of our project, then as the deadline came closer for submitting the completed manuscript for a playwriting competition, we met weekly. Sometimes for long hours.

A Dark Moon Writing Group met once every twenty-eight days on the particular day of the month that the new moon phase occurred, and for "Writing through the Months," participants came together for four hours on the last Saturday of every month for a full calendar year.

So frequency of meetings is determined by the group's purpose and agreement of the members. Coming together less than once a month can put a strain on the cohesiveness of the group. Of course, there's an exception to every "rule." I recall a vital and creative women's group that gathered every cross-quarter day of the pagan calendar for celebration, community, and writing. For a number of years they held eight events annually to honor the solstices, equinoxes, and other traditional festivals and the group remained strong and vibrant.

And for How Long?

Workshop also implies work, and participating in such events can be intense. You'll notice a palpable drop in the energy of the room toward the end of a three- or four-hour session; you can almost watch participants' eyes glaze over. Lots of yawning will be going on, too, though the work is stimulating. Even the air feels different — heavier and weighted with the aftermath of concentration and focus. After a daylong writing session of six or seven hours, marathoners sometimes experience a woozy lightheadedness — tired, yet still anticipatory. They report dreaminess and heightened sensory awareness, almost to the point of overstimulation. But a workshop of only an hour or two can leave participants vaguely dissatisfied and hungry for more.

As you determine how long you want your sessions to be, consider the intensity of the work. Anything that calls for lots of original writing can be as creatively stimulating as it is physically draining. Working to specific form, where more concentration is called for, can deplete energy much more rapidly than playful, no-holds-barred creativity. Writing that digs deep into an individual's emotional underpinnings is more exhausting than sailing

People-pleaser is one of those terms that hangs on from the recovery movement of the 1980s, back when everyone's family was dysfunctional and each individual had her own special dysfunction. The people-pleaser will change anything anybody wants or suggests, just so you'll think she's not contentious or hard to get along with. Oh, she wants you to like her. She wants it so much she's willing to sacrifice her own best ideas — or even her worst ideas — to yours, which must be better. The problem with the people-pleaser is not that she's so eager to please and anticipates what she thinks you (the big "you" of the universe) would like, the real problem is that she's so willing to give up her own voice. Writers by nature, and artists in general, cannot be people-pleasers. It's not our job to please. It's our job to tell the truth.

A writer with a chip on her shoulder is about as welcome as a Warning! Disk Failure notice on your computer screen. Why say anything when you know you're going to be challenged. Who told you that? Where'd you get that idea? Oh, yeah? Who said? The prove-it-to-me writer doesn't want to hear any of your ideas or thoughts, no matter how valid. The sound of her own voice is all this writer wants to hear, which makes her (or him) a real challenge in any writing group. Humor is a great defuser. Arguing or hefting a chip onto your own shoulders is not. You don't have anything to prove. You're just trying to be helpful and supportive.

free on the tides of imagination. Working with symbols and intuitive language takes more energy than focusing on the concrete, physical world.

No matter how long you decide to make your workshop, allow time for breaks and physical movement even if the only activity is that everyone stands and stretches after an hour or two. One workshop leader had us all up and performing jumping jacks during a particularly long session on a midsummer afternoon in a stuffy room. Another led us in stair climbs and deep knee bends. I often have participants change chairs after a while, just to change the perspective.

If you go for more than a few hours, you'll need to build in time for meals or some sort of refreshments. Something about doing all that creative work makes a body hungry. Crunchy food seems especially satisfying. Pretzels or carrots or popcorn and apples. And there will be those sweet-toothed writers who crave gummy bears or M&Ms. I've seen writers who otherwise never touch the stuff gnaw on red licorice as if it were good for them. And a box of Girl Scout cookies can be consumed in less time than an Olympic luge run down a mountain.

When planning your workshop schedule, be certain to take time for creating and nurturing community. And always, always, leave time for laughter.

Responding to the Work

Like the material created in the writing practice groups, the raw stuff of writing exercises in a workshop session may not be ready for critique. Sometimes the exercises result in just a phrase or two, a list of words or brief descriptions or paragraphs. Nothing that needs to be "critiqued." In other instances, the response of other writers can help a writer know if she's on the right path, or, if not, where she veered off.

One method of feedback is for participants to write down exact words or phrases to repeat back to the writer so he or she can hear what is working directly from listeners. In her book *Writing Personal Essays*, Sheila Bender calls these "Velcro words," or "words that stick." Writing guru Natalie Goldberg refers to this method as "say back." The listener says back to the writer exactly what she heard.

Rather than asking the writer what he intended to say, or telling him what they thought he meant, listeners are giving direct, nonjudgmental, specific, and immediate feedback. This method is different from read and critique, when participants are asked to offer opinions based on what they heard as they interpreted it through their own individual screening process. Read and critique is a valid, vital method of feedback, but not for raw, first draft material that has not first passed through the writer's own rewriting and editing process.

Sometimes I invite workshoppers to venture off the narrow path of actual, specific words and phrases to what they remember about the piece or what resonated with them. These comments may center around the mood of a piece, or the tone or attitude, or focus on a central theme or thread that runs through. The comments don't speak to what is lacking or what needs to be edited or fixed but instead offer an emotional reaction. The feedback isn't about the work itself so much as it is about the listener's response to what was written.

Another way of looking at the piece might be to ask what the listeners are curious about, what they want to know more about.

You'll notice that all of these methods of feedback tell the writer what is working in the material, not what still needs work. Any writer knows that this first, raw material will need editing and rewriting — sometimes a lot of it — and the writer should be given first crack at it, not readers.

If your group does want read and critique to be part of your work, build in time for rewriting between first efforts and first edited drafts.

"Creators need response, audience, sympathetic ears. But responding should never be confused with fixing."

— Sheila Bender

Types of Workshop Groups

Elements of Craft

Elements of the Craft are groups that focus on aspects of the craft of writing; for fiction or memoir writers it might be characterization, point of view, dramatic scenes, dialogue, and other components of the fictive voice. Poets would work with meter, rhyme, and form; metaphor and simile; imagery; voice and style. For those who write nonfiction articles or books, sessions could include the interview, leads, research, queries, and creative nonfiction approaches.

While some elements of each genre may be specific to that particular form, an excursion into another genre might offer up a change of scene that could be a broadening experience, like travel to a foreign country. Nonfiction writers who play around with figurative language might find their usually straightforward material sounding a bit more lively, and poets whose work may be too obscure can find someplace solid to ground themselves if they tread upon nonfiction's asphalt. A mixed genre workshop might be just the right blend of meat and cheese, pickles and onions.

Members can determine what elements they want to work on ahead of time, then a series of workshops can be developed. Early organizing meetings can be devoted to deciding the structure: participants list where they want to focus (characterization, for example, or dialogue) and the group can select an order, with assignments for planning the program taken by individuals. "I'll get us started on dialogue," Sandy might volunteer; "I'll do a session on scene," says Rowena. Participants can use exercises from craft books, material found online or from previous classes or workshops they've participated in. Books I've used include: *What If? Writing Exercises for Fiction Writers,* by Anne Bernays and Pamela Painter; two books titled *Writing from the Heart,* one by Lesléa Newman and the other by Nancy Slonim Aronie; *Turning Life into Fiction,* by Robin Hemley; *Making Your Words Work,* by Gary Provost; *Writing Personal Essays,* by Sheila Bender; *In the Palm of Your Hand,* by Steve Kowit; and dozens of others, some of which are listed in the Bibliography.

A program of an elements of the craft workshop might start with an overview or introduction. The person leading the workshop could begin with some quotes and read some examples before launching into the exercises. The number of exercises and the amount of writing/discussion time will depend on the length of the meeting. After each exercise, work will be read aloud, with discussion following.

How easy it is to let the discussion go to far and distant places and through all the meanders it wants, while no work gets done. So, a note

"It is helpful to me to pretend that writing is like building a house. I like to go out and watch real building projects and study the faces of the carpenters and masons as they add board after board and brick after brick. It reminds me of how hard it is to do anything really worth doing."

— Ellen Gilchrist

to the leader/timekeeper on the importance of keeping the train on the tracks. Otherwise you may find all your workshop time used up without ever leaving the station. Not a very productive trip.

Among other benefits of elements of the craft workshops, as all workshops where we roll up our sleeves and work alongside other writers, is the opportunity to learn from the experience of others. Give six people the same exercise — Write a poem in which you talk about anger without ever using the actual word — and each writer has the opportunity to hear six different approaches. You may learn as much from hearing Doreen's approach as you do from your own work. Or more. Sam's metaphor of the tree in a thunderstorm may open you to a way of seeing something (anger, metaphor, imagery, language) that you hadn't considered before. Always the opportunity exists to learn from other writers. The tendency to compare and analyze and judge our own work against that of others may always be present, especially for beginning writers or writers who are less experienced than their workshop mates. But it will not serve you. Most likely, you'll find more fault with your own writing, which won't feel good at all, and you'll miss the chance to really listen to the work of others to learn from it. The time for analyzing and judging your work and that of others, comes later, after you've had a chance to rewrite, edit, polish.

In an elements of the craft workshop, as in any workshop, writers can use the exercises to develop a work in progress. Playing around with dialogue by giving voice to the characters in their story or novel or creating a scene that might be set in their own project can serve double duty. They get to work on the craft and develop something that might find its way into a current project.

On the other hand, for writers not in the midst of a work, who knows what or who might appear on the workshop page? All practice, all writing is grist for the mill. Some of what we grind we get to take home with us and bake into a fine bread, and some is best left behind for the birds. But even at that, we become familiar with the sound of the grinding, the feel of the raw stuff in our hands. We come to recognize the smell of chaff in the air.

Sample Workshop Group Session

(This sample is for an Elements of Craft Workshop, but your group can adapt the program to fit most any type of meeting.)

1. Welcome and introductions (if needed)
2. "Call to workshop" (piece to begin session and set intentions, such as "The Artist's Creed" from *Marry Your Muse,* by Jan Phillips, or an inspirational quote.)
3. Introduction of topic (background information, quotes or examples)
4. Writing exercise(s)
5. Reading (follows each exercise)
6. Feedback (determine how feedback will be given)
7. Repeat of steps 3–6 depending on length of workshop
8. Discussions
9. Closure

Depending on the length of the workshop, breaks or lunch may be included in the schedule.

Exploring Your Voice

Could be you don't know what genre you want to write in or where your true voice rings. Maybe you've been working exclusively in one form and you're a little bored and long to see what lies beyond the gate. Workshops that form around explorations of voice and style can offer invigorating excursions for the inexperienced traveler as well as those who love to traipse in new territory. Topics for exploring your voice workshops might be "evoking the muse," "paths to creativity," "wild voice," "dancing with your shadow," "just get it down," or other sessions with equally stimulating titles. They're all designed to get the pen moving and the thinking/logical/judging mind out of the way of the creative/intuitive/imaginative mind.

These groups can meet regularly for a few hours each week, or every other week. The more often writers participate, the stronger the creative urge and the freer the pen. Too much time away tends to dull pencil point and fade ink. Creative joints get stiff and time must be devoted to limbering up all over again. Better to keep the writing body in shape with regular and frequent meetings. This will also engender trust, which goes a long way for those just finding their way. The more trust we feel in a group, the more risks we're willing to take.

Each session might open with a reading of a quote or statement of purpose. In the beginning people may be full of energy they've brought in with them; lively conversations abound as members greet each other and naturally want to catch up. The reading of an opening piece brings participants together, quiets the energy, and gives focus to the intention. As this "call to workshop" is read, a hush descends and calms the energy and brings the group to common purpose. For openings, I often read the "Guidelines for Writing Practice" (see page 108), or I may read a piece someone else has written, such as "The Artist's Creed" from Jan Phillips's book *Marry Your Muse,* or "The Basic Principles" from *The Artist's Way,* by Julia Cameron. Poems or inspiring quotes can serve the purpose. Your group may want to create its own preamble.

Exploring your voice groups never lose their excitement for me. I love the energy and the wild, freewheeling places the writing can take us.

The Artist's Creed

from *Marry Your Muse,* by Jan Phillips

I believe I am worth the time it takes to create
whatever I feel called to create.

I believe that my work is worthy of its own space,
which is worthy of the name Sacred.

I believe that, when I enter this space, I have the right
to work in silence, uninterrupted, for as long as I choose.

I believe that the moment I open myself to the gifts of the Muse,
I open myself to the Source of All Creation
and become One with the Mother of Life Itself.

I believe that my work is joyful, useful, and constantly changing,
flowing through me like a river with no beginning and no end.

I believe that what it is I am called to do
will make itself known when I have made myself ready.

I believe that the time I spend creating my art
is as precious as the time I spend giving to others.

I believe that what truly matters in the making of art is
not what the final piece looks like or sounds like,
not what it is worth or not worth, but what newness gets added
to the universe in the process of the piece itself becoming.

I believe that I am not alone in my attempts to create,
and that once I begin the work, settle into the strangeness,
the words will take shape, the form find life, and the spirit take flight.

I believe that as the Muse gives to me,
so does she deserve from me:
faith, mindfulness, and enduring commitment.

"The seeker, however, must seek — and this is the core of his difficulty. He cannot know what he is looking for until he finds it."

— William Segal

There is no end to the evocative prompts and props and techniques that can loosen tongues and pens. My own library of writing books serves as a banquet of writing feasts. I've learned from so many of these generous teachers and continue to add to the menu. Before an exploring your voice workshop or classes I teach, I set a day aside and lose myself among the pages. My books are littered with sticky notes and bookmarks. File folders list idea after idea that I've gleaned, or variations on the original ideas that have come as a result of trying out so many.

Among my favorites: *Poemcrazy*, by Susan Wooldridge; *Poetry Everywhere*, by Jack Collom and Sheryl Noethe; *Writing Yourself Home*, by Kimberley Snow; *The Observation Deck*, by Naomi Epel, *Finding What You Didn't Lose*, by John Fox; and of course, Natalie Goldberg's two classics, *Writing Down the Bones* and *Wild Mind*.

I also like to write from old photographs and postcards (sometimes I use scenes, sometimes people, sometimes choose one from each and put the character/person in the scene). Art books or cards. An ever-growing assemblage of found items that fill a basket or a box. Collections of boxes or rocks or jewelry or keepsakes. Cut-apart poems, sentence stems, slides, music, maps, guidebooks, recipe books, food. Use your wild imagination and creative discoveries to concoct evocative writing exercises.

Some of the ideas from the Write About a Day Moon: Prompts for the Writing Practice Groups section on page 103 and the Perfume Bottles and Darning Needles section on page 106 can be used for exploring your voice workshops. Encourage writers to write from the first person, using their own experience, or let characters' voices lead the way. Without giving specific direction, let the exercise suggest a poem or a monologue or a piece of fiction.

Each session of an exploring your voice workshop can include one or more writing exercises, depending on the length of the meeting and the stamina of the writers.

Writing exercises can go from 15 to 18 minutes (13 to 22, you choose). Or a series of short blasts: 3 x 3 x 3 x 3 x 3. Or a 17-minute write, followed fast upon by a 2-minute. The varying lengths of writing times encourage deep exploration as much as the different kinds of

"Literature thrives on abandonment of repression, a willingness to say anything, espouse, describe, and suggest anything at all."

— Scott Spencer

exercises. Vary the structure from week to week or workshop to workshop to keep things interesting and spontaneous.

And always, always, allow time given over to reading aloud. Not everyone will want to read after every exercise, but build in the time anyway. Six or seven writers reading the piece they created in a 17-minute exercise can take up to 20 to 25 minutes total reading time. Consider the amount of reading time as well as writing time as you construct your workshop.

Some participants might discover a fictive voice showing up again and again, with certain characters having their say. A story or scenes from a novel may begin forming on the page, or a series of personal narrative pieces with the common thread of a theme, maybe a cycle of poems. Your group may decide to include read and critique of pieces that find their way out of notebook and into manuscripted pages that have been edited and revised. This is a natural outgrowth of groups that nurture voice explorations. Enough poking around and trails are discovered, paths beaten down, and maps scratched out that lead to places that call for return trips. Maybe soon the construction of roads, landing strips. If/when this happens and participants feel the need for feedback on the work, you may want to include the practices of a read and critique group (see chapter 4). Like water finding the path of least resistance, writing groups follow a natural evolution. Finding your voice usually leads to telling your story and the need for form and context replaces the urge for random exploration.

> *"My advice is to hold your pen as if you are holding a small bird in your palm. Not so loosely that it flies away, not so tightly that you crush it."*
>
> — Philomene Long

Benefits of a Writing Workshop Group

- You learn something new or get to put into practice something you've only heard or read about
- Hands-on, sleeves-rolled-up experiential work
- You learn from the work performed and from the other participants
- Working in a group can be more fun than going it alone
- You get information that you can continue to use and translate into your own work

- You get feedback on the work you've done, and you get to hear feedback on others' work
- The exchange of information and experiences adds to your ever-growing satchel of knowledge
- You get to stretch your writing muscles and exercise your creative voice
- By spending time learning the craft and creating new material, you're developing your skills and honoring your writing self
- Meeting and interacting with other writers

Project Groups

Groups that come together to create a specific project, a performance piece or a play, or groups that create material for a chapbook may have a short but productive life. Generally when the project is complete, the group celebrates its success and disengages. Some of the members may want to stay together for another project, but the focus of this group is generally limited.

Among project workshops I've been a part of: a women's playwriting group that created a stage play which was performed by a local theater group. When the project was complete, we disbanded. The next year we came together again, only fewer of us this time — four instead of eight — and wrote another play, which was also performed. The third time around we attempted another group project, but for whatever reasons, it didn't work out and the group never worked together again, although one of the members did continue working on the play she started in the third session, completed it, and held a staged reading.

Another of my recurring workshop groups is Hot Nights, Wild Women, a series I've led three or four times. Twice we created a chapbook of the material produced in group, and presented readings. Each of the sessions included the return of some of the women as well as new writers. I enjoy that workshop group so much I may schedule another go-round.

"… success will more likely be the result of working with other people, and the same might be said of healthy self-esteem."

— Alfie Kohn

At The Writing Center, we presented several women's theater workshops that first developed the material then performed it as well as other groups that created chapbooks and held readings. These were staged at venues throughout the county: cafés, bookstores, libraries, museums (art, children's, natural history), retail stores, in the park, and outside on the street.

Other types of workshop groups included in this milieu are those that form around a book and work through the text together. There are scores of writing books that might seem a bit daunting to attempt alone, but that could turn out to be the perfect trail to lead a group on a fine creative outing. Suggestions: *The Writer's Idea Book,* by Jack Heffron (with more than four hundred writing prompts, this one will keep you off the streets for a while); *Writing from Life,* by Susan Wittig Albert; *Writing from Personal Experience,* by Nancy Davidoff Kelton; *Steering the Craft,* by Ursula K. Le Guin; and *The Poet's Companion,* by Kim Addonizio and Dorianne Laux.

How this type of group is structured will depend much upon the project or the book that is chosen. Still, some basic ground rules apply: the coming together, or the "call to workshop." This sets the scene and focuses the energy on the intention of the group. A group working through Anne Lamott's *Bird by Bird* might read something from that book, for example Wendell Berry's poem "The Wild Rose" that appears in the Introduction. A group developing a play could find something that related to the setting or characters. When my women's theater group, the Second Story Writers, was working on our first play, *Women of the Violet Wynn,* we began each session reading from a copied newspaper report or an excerpt from a book that had been written about the bordellos of the Stingaree District in early San Diego, which was the historical subject and setting for our piece.

Then comes the work itself: read and response (reading a certain text or writer, and writing in response to the material), freewriting or writing in real time (timed, focused writing exercises using prompts or topics), reading aloud, feedback (read and critique if it has been determined to be part of the gathering), followed by the "assignment,"

"Make sure you have other people in your life who will exert benevolent pressure to get you to keep writing."

— Anne Lamott

♀ ♂
Types of Writing Workshops

- Elements of craft focuses on specific aspects of different writing genres.
- Exploring your voice offers invigorating excursions into creative expression.
- Project groups come together to create a specific project or work through a text.
- Common Grounds workshops are structured around content that is specific to participants.

or what needs to be done before the next meeting, and any business that needs to be tended to. Finally, the social time, which may include the exchange of ideas or information, announcements, and, what we've all been waiting for, refreshments.

Of course, the order can be switched around. The social time can be at the beginning of the session, and the work of the workshop at the end. But I've found it best to use the tension that accompanies the anticipation of writing in doing the work itself, rather than allow the energy to dissipate through chitchat and noshing. Saved until last, conversation and food can feed the hunger whomped up by the work and relieve any leftover symptoms that might remain from the anxiety of doing it.

To structure the meetings, decide if participants will write material between gatherings and use the group's time for read and critique, or will the rough drafts of material be created in group, with rewrites and edits happening in between sessions? Will longer time elapse between get-togethers early in the project so writers have more time to create the new material, with the frequency increasing as the deadline nears? If there's to be a public reading, will time be spent at group sessions on rehearsing the material?

Workshop Ideas

Following are a few suggestions for workshop topics for elements of craft and exploring your voice workshops. There is no limit to where you can go and what you can explore. Let these few brief notes serve as starting points for your own creative ideas.

Elements of Craft

- Fiction — plot; dialogue; characters; setting; dramatic scenes; point of view; beginnings; middles and ends; conflict and tension; the story arc; fast fiction; the short short story
- Poetry — meter, rhyme, and form; voice and style; figurative language: imagery, metaphor, simile; styles of poetry:

narrative, sonnets, villanelles, sestinas; poetry of place; poetry of music; spoken word; found poetry

- Creative nonfiction and narrative nonfiction — memory as muse, stories of people and places, family stories, memoir, writing from life in the first person, writing the journey, coming-of-age stories
- Nonfiction articles and essays — finding the story; research; the interview; facts versus truth; putting people on the page; structure, voice, and style; permissions; how-to articles; travel articles; critiques and reviews; queries and proposals
- Show, don't tell
- Writing descriptions
- The telling detail
- Editing and revising
- Writing from the senses
- Voice and style

Exploring Your Voice

- Evoking the muse
- Wordplay
- Into the deep
- Writing wild
- Absolute beginners
- The sound of my voice
- Writing from the heart
- It's all copy — finding the stories from life
- What if...?
- Stories held by things
- Paths to creativity
- Memory as muse
- Voices of summer (or any of the seasons)
- First draft

Common Grounds

When writing about certain topics, writers may feel safer or freer to go deeper or to take more risks if other members of the group are swimming in the same waters. For example, issues related to gender, gays or lesbians, body image, HIV/AIDS, survivors of domestic violence, or other recovery groups. Also people within a certain age or life transition period may find their creativity stimulated by working with others who are writing from the same place. Knowing that you're with your own kind and surrounded by others who have some of the same experiences can create a powerful bond and also stimulate writing that goes beyond the borders of what might feel comfortable in other, more homogeneous gatherings.

While these groups might be structured along the same lines as any of the other workshop groups, focus and content set them aside. Referencing material by other writers who have worked in the same field for read and response and writing exercises that focus on exploration of all the hollows and ridges of specific topics can produce deeply felt and powerfully honest material. Writing can also be healing. Studies have proven that writing about traumatic or stress-related incidents or situations can stimulate T-cell production (T cells are the body's immune cells) as well as reduce stress-induced symptoms. Most regular journal keepers know the cathartic value of writing on topics that contain emotional pools and eddies. Writing helps us grieve that which needs to be grieved and heal that which still hurts.

Sometimes we may not even be aware that we are in need of working through some knotty emotional wood, until we recognize themes or images that repeat themselves in our writing. Our intuitive self knows what needs attention, even if our conscious brain or ego wants to set it aside, or dismiss certain thoughts or feelings. When you trust your intuition and the process of writing, remarkable things can happen. And often, it is easier to find the trust and to go through whatever pain or uncomfortable feelings that arise through the process when we are not alone.

If you have curiosities that call for examination, or if you feel tugs at the threads of what holds you together, try writing the questions. Find a group that is already in existence, or help create one of your own with like-minded writer friends. It always feels safer to walk past the graveyard in the company of another. Who knows when you might want to reach out to take a hand? Or when someone needs your warm clasp?

Other common grounds groups can form around family stories or cultural themes, bilingual writing, or racial or religious connectedness. In my community, for example, there exist the Taco Shop Poets, a group of Mexican-American writers; the African-American Writers and Artists Association; and the Asian-American Journalists Association. One friend and colleague who organized a gay men's writing group and an HIV/AIDS writing group continues to lead occasional "Writing from the Oracles" workshops for those who want to work with the tarot and other such divinators. Another associate formed an ongoing Women's Voices group that's been running for years. They produced several chapbooks and staged a number of readings. There was also the Men's Soul writing group, and Women Who Write with Children (But Would Like to Run with the Wolves). At The Writing Center we held teen and preteen workshops, a moms and daughters series, body image workshops, death and dying and grieving workshops, the poetry of politics and the politics of poetry.

Of course, like specialists who are so narrowly focused they not only miss the forest but see only one species of tree, diversities can be so diversified that it might be difficult to round up enough writers to make a group. The Bilingual Bisexual Lithuanians Whose Families Settled in Nebraska during the Great Potato Famine Writing Group, or some such silliness, might end you up with only yourself. And despite all the voices in our heads, one writer does not a group make.

"If you have curiosities that call for examination, or if you feel tugs at the threads of what holds you together, try writing the questions."

On a sheet of paper, make a list of questions. List those you have wondered in your head over and over, and those that come spontaneously. Write the questions you think you have answers to and the ones that frighten you most. Write the questions you are afraid have no answers.

✓ Workshop Group Checklist

Use this checklist to organize and structure your workshop group, or to help determine what type of workshop group yours will be.

- ❖ Type of workshop group
  - Elements of craft
  - Exploring your voice (or voice lessons)
  - Project workshop
  - Common Grounds workshop
  - Mix and match
  - Other
- ❖ Open/closed meetings
  - Will your group be open to the public or limited to membership?
- ❖ Membership
  - What are the criteria for membership?
  - Are there "duties" or "assignments" for members (secretary/program chair/etc.)?
- ❖ Frequency of meetings
  - How often will the group meet?
- ❖ Length of meetings
  - How long will the session be?
- ❖ Location
  - Where will the group meet (what are the criteria for meeting space)?
  - Are there special needs for the meeting place? Is setup required? Cleanup?
  - What about parking?
- ❖ Program
  - Who sets the program: program chair/rotating responsibility/volunteers?
  - What about input from group members?
  - Will there be special sessions with guest speakers or leaders?
- ❖ Facilitator/leader
  - Who leads the sessions?

❖ Structure of meetings
  • How will the meetings be structured?
  • Opening/closing
  • Breaks
  • Social time as well as "work" time?
❖ Materials
  • What materials are needed — books/texts/printouts/articles/reprints?
  • Other special materials
❖ Refreshments
  • Will there be refreshments? Who's responsible? What about cleanup?
❖ Fees
  • Will there be regular fees or dues? Materials fees? Fees for refreshments?
  • Who will collect/disburse?
  • Rent?
  • Honorariums/guest fees?
❖ Mailing list/phone list/e-mail list
  • Who will maintain the contact list?
  • Will there be regular contact?
❖ Publicity
  • How will membership/participation information be disseminated?
  • What about publicity for special workshops?
  • Ongoing listings/special notices
  • Web/e-mail contacts/listings
❖ Evaluations
  • How does the group evaluate itself? Its programming? Determine its future plans?

Not every group will want or need to have the detailed organization or structure this checklist implies. Don't let it scare you off. Still, even with a small group, it's a good idea to at least look over these notes if for no other reason than to anticipate possibilities and answer questions.

Profile: A Woman's Place — Stories, Poems, and Tall Tales of Women on the Road

One spring day the woman who was to become the organizer of this workshop stood in the crowded aisle of a travel store thumbing through destination books and recalling great trips she had taken and ones yet to come. *A Woman's World*, edited by Marybeth Bond, had just been published and the concept of women travelers writing their own stories struck the "what a great idea" chord. Why not gather together some local women travelers/writers and write our own stories?

She was a regular patron of the travel store and knew the owner, so when the "great idea" sounded, she thought maybe a reading of the work could be staged in the store. It could be a good promotion for the travel store and a cool addition to the workshop. When she asked the proprietor about the possibility of staging the reading, he suggested they hold the workshops in an upstairs meeting room.

"The concept of women travelers writing their own stories struck the 'what a great idea' chord."

That's how "A Woman's Place: Stories, Poems, and Tall Tales of Women on the Road," a workshop for women writers and travelers, came to be.

Word of the workshop was spread via mailings and word of mouth, and a workshop leader was recruited: Ashley Geist, who had more than a few miles under her well-worn walking shoes (she took part in the 1986 Great Peace March from California to Washington, D.C.), and was an experienced journalist as well as a fiction writer.

The workshop would be open to writers of all genres and would meet for six weeks over the summer, with the reading staged a few weeks after the completion of the workshop.

Twelve women signed up for the sessions. Travelers with myriad experience and diverse voices: a couple of poets, some creative nonfiction writers, a memoirist or two, and a handful of fiction writers.

For the first session, Ashley designed exercises that helped participants identify which specific journey they would focus on. Narrowing down the choices may have been the most difficult part of the whole workshop, especially for some of these writers who had traveled the world on all manner of conveyances, from cars to canoes to bicycles to trains and boats. These were not women who participated in organized tours or cruises.

Some came into the workshop expecting to write about one particular trip, but over the course of the exercises, a different story found its way onto the page. The exercises helped the writers find the adventures that held the most juice for them at that particular time. "Let the intuitive voice choose the story it wants to tell," was the gentle guidance of the leader. Content and form came out of the in-group exercises.

The space the store owner provided worked well for the structure of the workshops. The group met in a quiet and private upstairs room at long tables set up to accommodate all of them in one great spread. Still the exotic air of traveling and travelers curled up the stairs from the floor below. They met once a week in two-hour sessions. The first few sessions were devoted to generating new material, which was read aloud after each writing exercise. Later, when the material began to take shape into poems, essays, stories, and personal narrative, the participants split into smaller groups and meetings focused on read and critique. Time between sessions writers edited and revised the material, honing it to its final form.

Teri wrote a personal essay about a white-water canoe trip that "seemed like a great idea in the planning stages." Andrea created a heartwarming piece about how a young student in Paris became her guide for a day and taught her more about the kindness of strangers than she ever expected. Karin wrote about being in a car accident on Interstate 80 between Iowa and Nebraska, while Katarina's piece recalled her days as a student in Siena in 1989 — the difficulties of doing laundry and the delights of fresh baked bread. Corinne traveled the back roads of Pennsylvania with an octogenarian. Amy wrote about the time she and her sister trekked in Nepal, the siblings squabbling over Kleenex and hot water. A bike trip in the Unita National Forest with her best friend was the focus of Jane's piece; Karen created four poems that recalled places as far-ranging as a Minnesota bar, Mt. Rushmore, California's Highway 1, and the mountains outside San Diego. Lost

Workshop Flyer Notes

"Bring your memories, recollections, journals, and notes from journeys you've taken alone or with other women. . . .
Short short stories, poems, essays, personal narrative, creative nonfiction — the style is as wide-open as the spaces we travel."

loves and a long ride on the overnight train between Budapest and Split was the part-truth, part-fiction of Judy's piece. Sue found paradise in the Seychelles, and Nancy wrote about an Australian woman who chose a trip around the world instead of a down payment on a house. As well as leading the group in the writing exercises, Ashley wrote a short piece, too. The fear and exhilaration of flying in a small commuter plane to Flagstaff.

At the end of the six sessions, writers submitted their manuscripts for production of the chapbook, which was edited by Ashley and produced by one of the members with desktop publishing experience. The chapbook was not intended to be distributed to a wide audience; only a small number were produced. Each member of the group paid a small fee for copying and production costs.

A few weeks later the reading was held. Writers invited friends and family, copies of the chapbook were distributed, and amid the displays of maps and travel books and backpacks for sale, and among a gathering of friendly supporters as well as a few shoppers who stopped to listen, the women read their stories, poems, and tall tales.

7   BEYOND GROUPS

The Writer and the Larger Community

Just as becoming part of a writing group takes the solitary writer into the larger realm of community, there exist many opportunities for those who are curious and interested to reach even further — into a worldwide fraternity of writers or into their own backyards where by giving back to the community, the writer and his or her writing becomes an integral and vital part of it.

Writing Conferences and Retreats

Like writers themselves and the material they produce, writers conferences come in all shapes and sizes and all manner of description. From writing historical fiction in Taos to studying screenwriting in Manhattan, those who are looking to expand their writing community beyond their own backyard can choose from an offering of conferences as abundant as metaphors in a Tom Robbins novel.

At conferences, other interests and intents fall by the wayside and writing takes center stage. Writers can create fresh material, learn new skills, get manuscripts critiqued, participate in workshops, attend panel discussions, meet agents and editors, listen to readings, read their own work, discover new writers, study with the masters, party with peers, and generally immerse themselves in the writing life for a few brief days or weeks with like-minded others.

At some writing conferences, participants have an opportunity to "pitch" their project to agents or editors, or to schedule advance readings and one-on-one critiques with established writers. Many are the novels, books, and stories that have been published as the result of meeting between writer and agent or editor or publisher at the proving grounds of a writers conference. Mentor relationships have incubated beneath the shady branches of sycamores, in the fluorescent light of a classroom, or elbow to elbow in a crowded bar at two in the morning.

Whether writers are looking for a working vacation, a professional boost, or a meditative retreat, a simple search on the Internet (or in a few publications) can turn up a deluge of choices. So many, in fact, that just doing the research can take some serious time.

At the time of this writing, both the *Writer's Digest* and ShawGuides Web sites (www.shawguides.com or www.writersdigest.com) listed more than eleven hundred conferences and retreats in virtually every state in the union and in thirty-five additional countries. Want to write your memoir and go to Spain? Select La Serrania Retreats in Mallorca. Looking to study with someone like Yusef Komunyakaa? Check out the Prague Summer seminars. You can choose by genre — listings from autobiography to young adult, and including environmental and sci-fi along the way — or select by month, season, region of the country, or writer.

Poets & Writers magazine publishes an annual feature on conferences, offering expanded reviews and in-depth stories of several conferences written by writers who experienced them firsthand (see www.pw.org or the March/April issue of the magazine). The classified ad section in the back of every issue offers additional notices and information. Though not as current or as thick with listings as the *Writer's Digest* or ShawGuides sites, The Associated Writing Programs Web site offers extensive information about conferences presented by its member programs (see awpwriter.org).

Admission to some conferences is via advance submissions. Others don't require anything more than making a reservation, paying the fees, and showing up. Costs are as varied as the kinds of conferences and there may be additional fees to submit a manuscript for one-on-one

Not sure what you'd like from a conference? Do a five-minute freewriting beginning with "My ideal writers conference includes . . ." Give your imagination free rein and let your inner writer have her say.

critique. Size varies too, from the massive conference I attended one summer in Santa Monica (there were more than eight hundred of us) to the more exclusive retreats of ten to twelve attendees, and everywhere in between.

Consider attending a conference with other members of your writing group. It could be a great opportunity to share a different sort of writing experience together. At one summer conference, a quartet from our group roomed together in a nearby condominium. We shared meals and gossip and sunscreen, and the companionship and familiarity of old friends was as welcome as a hot bath at the end of the day. However, like traveling alone, going solo almost always means more conversations with strangers and instant friendships than when journeying with others. If one of the things you'd like to gain from attending such a gathering is to meet and interact with new people, going it alone may give you more opportunities. One writer I know continues to swap manuscripts with a man she met at a long-ago conference. They haven't seen each other in person again since their initial meeting, but their writing and correspondence continue to keep them connected and sustain a lively friendship.

So conference while you cruise (Murder Ahoy!), while you hike (Canyonlands Field Institute Writers Workshops), while you tour (Writing, Creativity and Ritual, Florence, Italy), or while you eat (La Dolce Vita Writer's Holiday). Go urban (Paris, New York, London), rural (Catskills Poetry Workshop), or wild (North Cascades Institute). Determine the features you want in a conference by going through the checklist on page 146 , then do a search to find which gatherings meet your criteria. Most of the conferences will have their own Web site, or you can request a brochure.

Searching for a Conference? Try the Internet

- www.writersdigest.com
- www.shawguides.com
- www.pw.org (*Poets & Writers* magazine)
- awpwriter.org (Associated Writing Programs)

Communities, Residencies, and Colonies

The idea of getting away to write is nearly as old as the idea of writing itself. Well, maybe not quite. But it's a familiar theme, enacted by writers since the days of St. John the Divine, who retreated to the isle of Patmos to pen Revelation.

✓ Finding the Right Conference

Use the following checklist to begin to identify what qualities you want in a writing conference. There are hundreds of conferences to choose from in virtually every state in the union plus dozens of other countries. With so many to select from, your problem might be in choosing just one. Good luck.

I want to create fresh material

I want to learn new skills and techniques

I want to get critique on my manuscript

I want to work with (specific type of writer or specific writer)

I'm interested in (specific genre or subject)

I want to study with some "masters"

I want to meet editors and agents

I want to "pitch" my project

I want to connect with other writers with similar interests

I'm ready for a vacation as well as work

I want to go on a retreat

The time of year that works best for me is _____

I want to travel as well as write

I want to explore my creativity

Here's how much time/money I want to spend

I'd love something big and crowded with lots of other writers

I'm looking for something small and intimate

I don't care too much about lodging, dorm rooms or rustic cabins are okay with me

Give me a bit of luxury or at least comfort for my money

These are just a few of the points to consider as you begin your research. Add your own "I wants" to the mix.

We sometimes need a retreat into a community where our work can be focused and undisturbed by the distractions of everyday life. Even in the best of situations, when we're able to seclude ourselves and work undisturbed for hours or days (and nights) on end, we occasionally need to immerse ourselves in the unfamiliar, to interact only with others who are similarly involved in their work. We need a place where our daily essentials are taken care of; we don't even have to prepare our own meals. Within the fine company of other creators we can produce our art, finish a project, work through a rough patch, or get a firm grasp on what eluded us in more familiar surroundings.

Writing colonies and residencies have existed in the United States since 1900, when financier Spencer Trask and his wife Katrina founded Yaddo in Saratoga Springs, New York. A few other artists colonies started in the early 1900s, and on the West Coast, Villa Montalvo in the Santa Cruz Mountains near San Francisco was established in 1930. Current listings on the Internet turn up more than three dozen such communities in the United States and another handful in Canada, Ireland, France, Mexico, and other countries.

Most colonies are small and accommodate only a handful of writers at one time. Some offer private rooms or studios, a community room, and lovely, spacious grounds often in secluded, tucked-away environments. If there are any fees, they are often very low ($15/day at Ragdale, a retreat in Lake Forest, Illinois, or $125/week at Hambridge, which is located outside Atlanta, Georgia). Some communities also offer stipends and fee-reduced scholarships. Residencies vary from a few weeks to a few months. To apply for admissions, writers may be asked to submit work samples, a statement about their work in progress, referrals, and a résumé.

Applications for residencies such as Ragdale, Yaddo, or most other writers colonies far exceed acceptances. It's competitive and though it's not always the experienced versus the inexperienced writer who is accepted, an established and evident commitment to the craft as well as the quality of the work weigh in the choices.

Some centers that are more retreat than residency don't have

"Find the time to write. Protect the time to write. Be inventive: get gorgons. Forget e-mail. Whatever it takes. Because you'll still need more time than there is, and also it's important to leave enough time to waste."

— Ann Beattie

stringent acceptance criteria. A writing sample, letter of recommendation, and the appropriate fee can reserve a room or a studio for a weekend, a week, a month, or longer. Sometimes all you need is the fee. Costs range from moderate to pricey, depending upon the accommodations and meal service.

For more information about writing communities, select "Colonies, Residencies, & Retreats" on the ShawGuides Web site. *Artists and Writers Colonies: Retreats, Residencies, and Respites for the Creative Mind*, edited by Robyn Middleton, Mindy Seale, Martha Ruttle, and Stacey Loomis, is another resource for listings.

Professional Associations and Groups

Professional organizations offer writers opportunities for support, information, education, training, and association with like-minded people and a collective voice. Other benefits may include special conferences and gatherings, publications such as newsletters and, more than ever before, Web sites. Local chapters of national organizations as well as smaller, local groups hold regular meetings with guest speakers or panels and organize workshops, retreats, or conferences. Those looking for a writing group may be able to find others similarly interested within the membership of a professional organization.

Becoming a member of a professional organization can offer the benefits of community to an individual writer and beyond that, such associations add to the quality of life for the entire community. More Art = Better Living. It goes without saying.

Open Readings

It's Tuesday night and the mike is open at Claire de Lune Coffee Lounge. Poets from all over the county choose their best stuff (or the stuff they want to try out or work on or just speak out loud), and take to the stage. Sandwiched on either side of the featured poet, fifteen or eighteen poets will recite or read or perform their work in increments of five minutes each. Jazz and hip-hop and political and confessional and

A Few Organizations

- Romance Writers of America
- Society of Children's Book Writers and Illustrators
- Sisters in Crime
- Horror Writers
- Science Fiction and Fantasy Writers
- Society of Women Writers and Journalists
- International Black Writers and Artists
- SPAWN (Small Publishers, Artists, and Writers Network)
- PEN, which is a "fellowship of writers working . . . to advance literature, to promote a culture of reading and to defend free expression."

narrative and even some of the classic forms — sonnets and sestinas or quadrilles and maybe a haiku or two.

Somewhere around 11 P.M. the host will thank everyone for coming, remind us to take care and to keep writing and we'll all go home full of words and images and energy. Maybe write a poem when we get there. Or maybe we won't go home. Maybe we'll cruise the freeway to L. A. and back, write a poem about that, and say it next week.

It's the same and not the same in venues all over town. In my city and communities across the country and in countries around the world. Open readings, which are often called open mikes, have a long and passionate history. The first may have been the Theater of Dionysus in ancient Greece, where poets recited their work and the first lyrical plays were performed.

Open readings aren't just for poets. For the duration of its too-brief life, we staged Third Sunday Open Readings at The Writing Center. There, among the litter of wooden tables and chairs and The Writing Center cats, Lily and Emily, who roamed from lap to lap, creators of fiction, nonfiction, poetry, and all genres of writing gathered to read their work. Not just completed work either; open readings are a great place to read works in progress, and not for critique or feedback, but to hear it for yourself. Always, the words sound different read out loud and before an audience than at home in your study with only your own jaundiced hearing. Discoveries are made at open mikes, and secrets revealed from pages you thought you knew so well.

Open readings are a great place to meet other writers, too. Attend one for a while and you'll become part of a fluid community that forms and reforms at every gathering.

Each open reading will have its own personality. The host, the participants, and certainly the venue influence the ambiance. A dimly lit café with people elbow to elbow at tiny, crowded tables, the buzz of caffeine electrifying the place, feels a whole lot different than a sunny Sunday afternoon in the park, writers sprawled on blankets or flimsy folding chairs, all hats and sunglasses, or the gathering of readers amid

"It seems to me the most integrative social power contained in words is liberated in performance.... For me, it is the activist and spoken element which follows on the contemplative act of composition which is most capable of vitalizing folk."

— Adrienne Rich

the tall, laden shelves crowding the aisles of a bookstore where browsers may or may not eavesdrop as the readings progress.

Strict guidelines or loose, almost always there will be a time limit set for readings and an order for readers that can be as spontaneous as a lottery or as methodical as numbered sign-ups. At our Third Sundays, we listed numbers from one to fifteen on the sign-up sheet and people could more or less choose their order. Often the evening started with reader number three or four because no one wanted to be the first up.

If you plan to read at an open mike rehearse the piece aloud and time yourself before taking to the stage. Exceeding the time limit is more than just impolite; it's usually viewed as unacceptable. It's also good manners to stay for the entire reading, and not just do your own thing then head out for a cold one. Show your appreciation and support for other writers by paying attention during their readings. Make a point to tell a writer when you enjoyed her work. Be specific.

Like public art, open readings are for everyone. And like public art, readings stimulate dialogue, create connections, evoke passion, and nurture creativity. The size of the audience or the depth of participation or even the quality of the work is not the measure of the success or value of an open reading. The community that encourages and nurtures self-expression of its members, diverse and unwieldy as it may be, will be the richer for it.

"The community that encourages and nurtures self-expression of its members, diverse and unwieldy as it may be, will be the richer for it."

"Come on Kids, Let's Put On a Show"

Staging an open reading isn't all that different from setting up and running a group or a workshop. You'll need a time and a place, some kind of structure to hold the thing together, and publicity. If it's to be an ongoing event that will need continued organization, publicity, and follow-up, doing it with a little help from your friends is always easier (and more fun) than going solo. This may be a good project for your group.

Attend a few open readings to see how others do it. When you're on the road or visiting another community, check out the local open mikes. Bringing back ideas from other places is a little like returning home with a gift. Think of it as a literary T-shirt.

Do some research before you decide the day and time so you don't compete unnecessarily with other events that might be vying for the same audience. Weekday nights are best, though Sunday evenings can work too. Consider a spring or summer series on weekend afternoons staged out-of-doors. Readings beneath the waxing moon on summer nights with twinkle lights aglow have a festive, maybe even romantic, ambiance.

Look for a venue that suggests the kind of setting you want to create. A bookstore on a Monday evening, chairs arranged cozily near the poetry section. Ask your local bookstore if you can hold an open reading in their space. Some bookstores post flyers and list open readings in their calendar of events and on their Web sites. Maybe your idea of the right place is a local café where you can be the entertainment for the evening. If there's a charge for room use, a donation basket can be passed or a small entry fee may be necessary. As a rule, sign-up fees for open readings are discouraged.

Determine the length of time for each reader. Up to five minutes if you've got a crowd and the work is mostly poetry. Ten, if participation is made up of fiction and nonfiction writers. Decide how you'll manage the time — will you have a timekeeper? will you have a system for letting readers know when their time is up? — and the process of choosing the order. With a smaller group, a sign-up sheet serves the purpose; more people and another, more random method may be necessary. Names in a basket or two-part tickets, which lend spontaneity to an event. Interesting, also, the juxtaposition of subjects and delightful synchronicities that can happen when you allow chance to have her influence.

The same methods of publicity can work for getting the word out about open readings as suggested for publicizing a new group or a workshop (see chapter 3, page 21). One of the reasons for the tremendous success of the Poetic Brew open readings at Claire de Lune (in addition to having a feature poet and all that great energy and supportive environment) is the e-mail newsletter Cheryl Latif originated when she started the series. Current host Marc Kockinos continues to send weekly e-mail announcements of the feature along with a lively report

"Just as you would reach your most moving line, somebody would be sure to either turn on the espresso machine or flush the toilet and open the door... these things just happen — a lot — and you have to handle them as they come along. I think white-water canoeing is really good practice for that."

— Margaret Atwood

of the readings of the previous week and other news and notes of interest. Anybody and everybody can get on the mailing list; all they have to
do is sign up. All this organizing and publicizing and staging the event
takes a great amount of volunteer time and creative involvement. More
reasons that I view open readings such as Poetic Brew as gifts writers
give to the community.

✓ Putting On an Open Reading — List of Ingredients

❖ Time
- Weeknight, weekend afternoon or evening
- Every week, once a month, occasionally
- Length (two hours, three, more/less)

❖ Place
- Café, bookstore, performance space, community building, museum, library, outdoor space

❖ "Voice"
- Style, theme, focus, genre (what are the values you want to bring to your open readings and what audience do you want to reach?)

❖ Program
- All open mike or feature reader plus open mike
- Time allowed for each reader
- Order of readings

❖ Spreading the word
- Publicity
- Mailing list, both e-mail and U.S. mail

"Everyone Is Talented, Original, and Has Something Important to Say"[1]

One of my most popular workshops is "Finding Our Voices, Telling
Our Stories." The catalogue description begins, "Within each human

1. This phrase is from Brenda Ueland, *If You Want to Write* (St. Paul, Minn.:
Graywolf Press, 1996).

being dwells an innate sense of storytelling and each of us has a unique voice with which to tell our stories." I'm certain that what makes this course so popular is that this first line resonates with people, who recognize that they have stories to tell — oh, do they have stories! — but they've yet to discover the voice with which to tell them, or found a way to express that voice.

Often all people need is someone to encourage them, someone who will show them how to get what's inside out. *Try this. Try this. Try this.* I've seen folks so full of what they want to say they can hardly sit still and others who are so shy and introverted they believe their stories aren't important. "Who wants to hear about that?" they ask. "I do," I tell them. Still others may not think they have anything at all to say.

One of the most fulfilling ways a writer can give back to the community is by volunteering his time and sharing his experience with others, either one to one or within a group. Encouraging others to tell their stories through writing, and supporting them in finding and expressing their voice can be as healing for the writer as it is for those being helped. It's good for the planet, too.

Writing Groups in Shelters, Treatment Centers, and Other Closed Communities

I have seen firsthand the powerful effect writing can have on people who are grieving a great loss and those recovering from alcoholism or drug addiction. I've been in homeless shelters when stories get written and through the alchemy of finding the words and putting them on paper, long-standing walls turn to dust. Tough girls whose defenses are brittle as the chipped polish on their silicone nails allow themselves to be vulnerable on the page, and the stories of beaten down women become the truth in the act of writing them down. "This is what happened," they say, self-esteem and confidence elevated with each word they pen. And I've read the wildly creative constructions of mental health patients who finally access a voice that can carry their self-expression.

Writers who lead groups behind the locked doors of jails tell of touching and honest poems, intimate narratives, and tender stories

"Encouraging others to tell their stories through writing, and supporting them in finding and expressing their voice can be as healing for the writer as it is for those being helped."

of love and loss. There's anger, to be sure. Rage on paper so volatile it could spontaneously combust. And humor and raw, ragged emotions wrapped in words as powerful and charged as lightning on the plains.

And there, in the quiet garden of a hospice overlooking the deep valley below, confessions and secrets and lost dreams and regrets and forgiveness and memories and prayers are shaped from whispered pen to open page.

Not for everyone, this work of writing with others in such settings or others equally intensive and prone to emotional intimacy and exposure. But if you or members of your writing group are willing and able and can find a way, the rewards are vast. Most writers who become involved in this kind of service ultimately touch deeper and more profound reaches in their own work and perhaps, more important, within their own beings.

Putting Moonbeams in a Jar

Capturing the energy of children and harnessing it to the page is not all that different from the Wild Mouse ride at the fair. From the ground it looks tame enough, a few tight curves and loop-the-loops, but, come on, it's not the roller coaster. Get aboard and it's a whole different story. Flung this way and that, one neck-wrenching turn after the other, and you're exhilarated and half scared at the same time. And finally, when it's all over and the little car has come to a stop, you're grinning like a fool and you want to do it all over again.

Writing with kids is that kind of adventure. Sometimes.

Other times they're pouty and reluctant and distracted and getting them to write is like trying to get gum off the sole of your shoe.

Still, helping young people find and express their voice is a lively and rewarding and challenging experience — for you and for them.

Opportunities to work with children can be found in the schools (many states and cities sponsor Writers in the Classroom series), through community centers, the Y, Boys and Girls clubs, or through the city parks and recreation department, public library, or any number of nonprofit or service organizations. Often you need look no further

---

"You can bring any fine arts in front of children, but when you deal with words, you scratch the soul."
— Fr. Amde Hamilton,
Watts Prophets

than your own backyard. There might be a whole band of budding writers out there right now. I've also worked with kids through Scouts and Campfire groups, churches, museums, and at The Writing Center, where we sponsored summer writing camps.

Many good books about writing with youngsters are available. One of my favorites is *Poemcrazy,* by Susan Wooldridge. I also use this book for my own work. It's a delight. Others, such as *Poetry Everywhere,* by Jack Collom and Sheryl Noethe and *The Writing Workshop,* Volume I and II, by Alan Zeigler, are available through Teachers & Writers Collaborative, which has an extensive list of such publications (see www.twc.org).

Tales from the Long Highway

The stories we write when we're kids are often fantasies and nonsense and wild imaginings. At the other end of the long highway are the tales we tell when we are older, much older. These are the stories of experience and memory, populated with those we have known over a lifetime and those we have lost. The stories of seniors are commonly of times gone by and unless they have a chance to tell us, times soon forgotten. Nowhere does it become more obvious that "each of us has a story to tell" than at a gathering of the elderly. And, sadly in our culture, less and less often does anyone want to hear these stories.

You can be the one to listen. You and your writing group or one or two of your friends. Take pens and notebooks to circles of seniors and give them a chance to tell their stories. Offer your time and guidance at senior centers or residential homes. A wealth of books and guides are available for working with those who want to write stories from their lives (not that this is the only kind of writing that would be of interest for these groups). I've used both Lois Daniel's *How to Write Your Own Life Story* and Frank Thomas's *How to Write the Story of Your Life.* These days, I work without a net and make it up as I go, using the techniques of writing practice and topics that work as memory sparkers.

Taking a group of young people to a senior center where everyone — young and old alike — gets to share can touch people in ways you

Not sure what type of group or in what setting you'd like to volunteer? Start with the prompt, "These are the voices I'd like to hear..." and freewrite for five minutes. Do another freewriting using the prompt, "These are the stories I'd like to hear..." Do this exploration by yourself or invite your writers group to join you.

might not expect. Our stories have always been what connect us as human beings. It's in our DNA.

Gifts to the Community

My grandmother told me that when we were being formed, God put His big thumb right between our eyes and imprinted us with what we were to be. "You're a singer," He might've said to my friend Peggy, whose beautiful voice thrills me. "You're a potter," He said to my sister Jackie, who spends entire days bent over her wheel. "You make people laugh," He told my daughter, who performs stand-up comedy. And to me and you if you be one, He said, "You're a writer."

Whether or not I believe my grandmother's story (how I loved to imagine it when I was a young girl, looking for the whorls and spirals of some great fingerprint on the forehead of every one I met), I do believe that each human being has a gift of self-expression that is creative and unique. Not all of us are singers (nowhere is the absence of this gift more obvious than in my own case), not all of us are potters or comedians. And not all of us are writers. But all of us are human beings with the need to express our unique selves in the world, in our own unique ways, and what a richer place it is for all of our many and various expressions.

A companion belief I hold is that each of us has a responsibility to use our gifts for the betterment of all. This is how we evolve, with each of us giving back in our own original and creative way. Our contribution to the whole raises us as a species to a higher level.

And so as we toil away in our solitude, writing and writing, we make the world a better place by being true to ourselves and responding to our deepest creative urgings. At this level, our contribution is in living an authentic life. When we give this writing to the world we make an offering of what we have created. By joining a writing group we contribute on a more personal plane. Not only are we offering our writing, we are now giving ourselves — we support other writers and share our knowledge and experience. And when writers individually or as a group bring

"What we do with our lives individually is not what determines whether we are a success or not. What determines whether we are a success is how we have affected the lives of others."

— Albert Schweitzer

the gift of writing to the larger community, we are, in a way, bringing it home. "The people, and not the college, is the writer's home," wrote Ralph Waldo Emerson.

From staging writing festivals to creating literary centers to participating in street fairs or any of a hundred involvements, writers' contributions to the community bring the words to life and add life to the words.

Following are some ideas for writers who want to take it to the streets. Some of the projects can be done with not much planning and even less money; others will require organization and funding that may take some time to gather. You may have to start small with the intention of expanding as you get more involvement and more sponsors.

- Set up booths at street fairs and create an ongoing story with passersby contributing characters' names or plot twists. Offer to write poems on demand.
- Choose a noteworthy day to honor a writer. Every Halloween at the Writing Center we staged the E. A. Poe Memorial Benefit and Wake with contests for scary stories and readings of Poe's stories by local actors and performers. Celebrate Bloomsday with continuous readings of James Joyce's *Ulysses* on June 16 as is done in towns and cities around the world. Maybe there's a hometown author you'd like to celebrate.
- Many construction sites invite local schoolchildren to paint murals on their fences. Why not ask if you can create a written mural? Invite writers and artists to cocreate the design.
- Some cities integrate poetry into the mix of public service messages and advertising that ride along top of the windows inside their buses. Find out how you can bring such literary signage to your community's public transportation.
- Create your own "Moveable Feast" of writing as writers stage readings in locations around the community. Do it at

Literary Gifts to the Community

- Set up "writing" booths at street fairs and community celebrations
- Choose a noteworthy day to honor a writer
- Create a written mural on a construction site fence
- Put literature in motion on your city's public transportation
- Create your own "Moveable Feast" by staging readings at locations around town
- Produce a poetry or literary festival
- Offer tours of the literary history or literary geography of your town
- Create a community anthology; invite everyone to submit
- Stage a literary fundraising event for a local charity
- Plant a "poetree" on Arbor Day

trolley stops and in parking lots, outside baseball stadiums and beneath bridges. Under a spreading chestnut in the park and in a pavilion next to the river. You can select the readings to complement the place, or not. Invite people along for the complete tour, or do the readings spontaneously without announcement or fanfare. Like the "happenings" we used to create in the sixties.

- Produce a poetry or literary festival. Invite a well-known writer or two to read and include work by local community members. Sponsor a writing contest for schoolchildren as well as seniors and everyone in between.
- Discover the literary geography or history of your community and offer tours. Maybe not every town has a Cannery Row or a Tom Sawyer fence, but every town has something of literary interest somewhere. If it doesn't, create one. Sponsor an event for writers to feature a local attraction or icon in a story.
- Create a community anthology by inviting people from the entire area to submit material. When the book is completed, organize a reading to bring everyone together to celebrate themselves and the project.
- Stage a fundraising event for a local charity — the public library, a nonprofit literacy organization, or a community arts project, maybe even one that you organize. Present a special reading with well-known authors or have a marathon writing or reading event in which participants get sponsors to support their efforts (by the word or the hour).
- Plant a "poetree" on Arbor Day and stage an annual reading on the site.

These are only a few suggestions. Turn your group's limitless and generous imagination loose and create your own literary gift to your community.

Profile: Recovering Alone, Recovering Together

This is the story of one writer's work with recovering alcoholics and addicts during the two years she led a writing group at a long-term residential treatment facility. With respect for the anonymity of the individuals she worked with and wrote with, she asked to remain anonymous.

The group began in the fall, golden mornings of driving through citrus groves and avocado ranches into the low mountains of San Diego's backcountry. In her pack on the seat beside her, a blue three-ring binder with notes and session plans, copies of handouts, and her own notebook. She said she always wrote along with the group. As much participant as leader, her own writing took her to those same deep and sometimes scary and often tender places of discovery and recovery the others experienced.

Ten or twelve men and women, late teens to upper seventies, some in early recovery, others further along, residents at the facility for six or eight months. The center specializes in treatment for relapse-prone alcoholics and addicts. She is a recovering alcoholic, too. For her, it is a way of giving back, to both the recovering community and as a gesture of service for what she considers the gift of her writing.

She doesn't remember exactly how the group came about. Did she make the offer to the director of the treatment facility or did the director invite her? Either way, it was a good idea. With her experience in leading writing groups and her background in recovery, it seemed a natural. And maybe that's the way it came about; it just happened naturally.

Every other Monday morning from 10:00 until 11:30, the group gathered around the big round wooden table in the dining room, notebooks spread before them, and wrote together. Sometimes they would start with a meditation before they wrote their first entry. Or she would explain a particular exercise: how to use clustering or how to keep a daily log or write an unsent letter. Other times she would simply offer up a topic, "This morning I thought about _____" or "I remember _____." She'd set a time for the writing, giving the group ten

"Creativity called for all the things the convent had call for — solitude, prayer, a sense of community, and a commitment to service. In order to create, I had to find that balance, and when I had it, joy returned."

— Jan Phillips

or fifteen minutes to do the exercise. And, following each writing, participants were invited to read aloud.

Like so many other groups where personal writing is the focus, there was no critique on the material that was read. Just acknowledgment for the work and sometimes a comment from the leader that offered support or a suggestion to do some follow-up writing on a particular spot that seemed "hot." The writers learned to search their own work to find such places and during the time between sessions reviewed what they'd written, expanding or going deeper. She also gave them assignments to work on over the two weeks before their next meeting.

Writers also learned that what was written in group was private, not to be talked about with other residents or with the staff, and they learned not to ask questions about a particular piece of writing or to pry into something that had been revealed during the session. What was shared in the group stayed in the group. Respect for the sovereignty of the writing became an unspoken guideline. What freedom! To be able to write and speak anything you want without concern that you might offend someone, or have to defend or explain or take back what you wrote. You just turn yourself over to the process, tell the truth, and keep writing.

"It's your experience and you get to write about it any way you want. No one is going to censor you or correct you or scold you," she told group members. On occasion, especially if they were new, participants might try to shock the others or get a rise out of the leader. Or they'd use their writing to rage or vent. But when they realized no one was shocked, no one reacted, and most of all, the leader didn't take stories out of the group to the staff — in other words when they learned they could trust the group and their own voice — they settled into the work of the writing and used it as another tool for recovery.

Much of the writing was journal writing, rather than creative writing, though who can say where one stops and the other begins, each carrying traces of the other. Some poems and stories were created, but mostly the writing focused inwardly. Memories surfaced, old stories and lies and unrealized truths. Hurts forgotten or buried until the writing revealed them again.

"... I often feel as though I'm taking part in a much larger conversation, one that reaches back as far as Athens and has kept the lamp burning in many windows down the centuries, wherever young writers have gone for advice, for inspiration, for 'correction' and — of course — for love."

— Jay Parini

"During the two years of the group there may have been as much Kleenex used as writing paper," she said. "I was honored that participants would trust me and the group enough to go to those deep and vulnerable places, to do the writing and then have the courage to read out loud what they had written," she said. "Everyone healed as a result of the work of each individual."

There was laughter too, same as with any group of writers. "We tell our stories and we laugh at ourselves and laugh with each other." Laughing together also has a way of healing. Maybe that's why they call it the "best medicine."

Finally, after two years of working and writing with the group she had to let it go. A day job that wouldn't allow her to continue her Monday morning trips to the mountains. She said she still has her blue binder, "all beat up and raggedy at the edges." She found within its shambled leaves, pages from her own notebook, their scrawly lines and scratched out words. "Look," she said, "evidence of a writer writing."

A P P E N D I X

Online Groups

Like zucchini in July, online writers groups are proliferating beyond any word gardener's expectations. Web sites, e-groups, message and bulletin boards, e-newsletters and e-zines, links and rings — there are so many sites it would take a book the size of the Manhattan telephone directory to collect them all. And like any phone book, many of the numbers would be incorrect and the listees long gone by the time it got to print. So, rather than attempt to create a current list of online groups, this appendix discusses a few of the different types of groups and how to find them, and explores the upside and the downside of electronic writing communities.

Just to get an idea of the amazing numbers of possibilities, go to any search engine (such as Yahoo! or Lycos or Google) and type the key-words "writing" or "writer's groups" or "writers" in the subject line. You'll be bombarded with so many offerings it can make your keyboard vibrate and your mouse tremble at the sheer immensity. And anyone who spends any time searching or surfing the Web knows how time-consuming it can be. Talk about your time warps. I've seen day pass to night and back to day again while being held mesmerized by the infinite choices of the Web. Your best bet may be to go to the *Writer's Digest* Web site (www.writersdigest.com) and check out their "Top 100 Websites." Submitted by the editors, staff, and contributors of *Writer's Digest* magazine as well as readers and Web writers, the annual lists

"Online writers' groups provided much needed camaraderie and professional writing advice."

— Lynn Alfino

cover a wide range of writing and literary information, Web sites, and groups. You can search by topic or view the entire list, A–Z. Once inside some of the Web sites, you'll find more listings and links to other sites.

Want to take an online workshop? Hundreds of them are offered. Want to read what professionals have to say about the art and craft? Writers from John Irving to Joyce Carol Oates to Kurt Vonnegut are listed. Many have their own Web sites. Looking to get critique or feedback on a story or poem or article? Easy-to-find places to post your e-manuscript where you'll receive helpful and objective and thoughtful comments. (A bounty of not so helpful or objective or thoughtful commentary, too.) Discussions, dialogues, questions and answers, tips, hints, guidelines, counsel and advice, support, inspiration, promotion, jobs, contests, articles, instruction, even visitations from the e-Muse — all these are available anytime, day or night, and, with the exception of some online workshops and classes, all for free.

Join a poetry group, talk with writers of your own kind (specialty and genre groups abound) in chat rooms, offer up your critique of others' work, and create a piece to online prompts along with who knows how many other writers from around the globe. There are groups for teens and women and kids, ethnic and cultural groups, groups for Christians and pagans, moms and students, life-story writers and journalists. You can find funding for writers and listings of writers conferences and retreats and other gatherings. You can even start your own online writers group. What a great opportunity to interact with writers from far-flung and distant places! An especially great opportunity if you're from one of those remote places and haven't been able to find other writers with whom to connect.

Though there are live chat rooms and message boards where you can post your comments, much of the online group activity is conducted via e-mail. Once you join, you send and receive messages, manuscripts, or comments. In the online workshop I led, all communication was through e-mail correspondence. I posted the lessons and "handouts" and the students e-mailed their assignments to me. I made comments and sent them back via e-mail. In this case, the students didn't have access to one another's writings, though in other online workshops and groups, they do, and they're invited, or sometimes required, to comment on the work. Some workshops offer live chats with all the participants online simultaneously. Lively discussion and debate spring from this virtual interaction of group members.

What online groups have to offer are some of the same qualities you'll find in a "live" group: communication and interaction with other writers, the opportunity to share writing and to give and receive support, to be exposed to other writers' work and process, and to have an audience and to receive feedback.

What online groups lack is the live, in-person connection that a real-time writing group offers. The community that is built online is not as intimate or personal as the community that evolves from people coming together in person. So much is carried in the sound of a voice, in physical expression, the out-loud laughter, or "holy silence" that fills a room after a particularly powerful piece is read aloud. It's good for us to see and touch one another, to make eye contact, and to share space and air and food together. How do we measure the value of giving and receiving smiles or glances that let us know we're understood?

A common complaint about online groups is blunt and sometimes harsh critique. (Not to mention the nattering on of some critiquers or the repetition of comments.) Though most sites have rules against "flaming," it still happens. And, because of the anonymity and vacuum of online communications, what might be considered straight-ahead, no-nonsense critique in a live group can come across as brusque and sometimes downright mean-spirited in an online group. Words spoken aloud when people are face-to-face in a friendly, supportive environment can sound less brutal than words keyboarded into an e-mail message (often with misspellings and grammar errors, to boot). When you can't see a person's face, you can't tell how your words are affecting her. Also, clarity is sometimes lacking in online communiqués, and what might be cute or funny or witty in person may come across as sarcastic in an e-mail; what was intended as a joke might be taken seriously.

"The nice thing about cyberspace is its vastness. If you don't feel comfortable with a particular group, with just a few keystrokes you can join another. You should always come away from your group feeling inspired to write. If you don't, start surfing."

— Raymond Obstfeld

Other drawbacks: It's easier to go missing in an online group than it is in live groups. There's usually no accountability so membership and "attendance" can be spotty. Consequently, the level of commitment may be lower than that of in-person groups. This certainly isn't always the case, or even most often the case. Many online groups have as steady and committed a membership as any other sort. But online, it's much easier to drop in and drop out. This fluidity can be disconcerting to the individual members and play havoc with attempts at community building.

I don't want to sound as though I'm not in favor of online groups or virtual writing communities. I am in favor of them. But I'm also very sensitive that, out of necessity, we writers must isolate ourselves and spend so much of our time in solitary. (Oh, the passivity of television screens and computer monitors.) We need more than virtual interaction, we need live, in-person connection with others of our own kind. We need it for balance and perspective and growth. We need it for warmth and nurturing. This connection is as essential to us as sunlight and as natural as love.

BIBLIOGRAPHY

Addonizio, Kim, and Dorianne Laux. *The Poet's Companion: A Guide to the Pleasures of Writing Poetry.* New York: Norton, 1997.

Albert, Susan Wittig. *Writing from Life: Telling Your Soul's Story.* New York: Tarcher, 1996.

Allen, Roberta. *Fast Fiction: Creating Fiction in Five Minutes.* Cincinnati: Story Press, 1997.

Aronie, Nancy Slonim. *Writing from the Heart: Tapping the Power of Your Inner Voice.* New York: Hyperion, 1998.

Baldwin, Christina. *Calling the Circle: The First and Future Culture.* New York: Bantam, 1998.

Bender, Sheila. *Writing Personal Essays: How to Shape Your Life Experiences for the Page.* Cincinnati: Writer's Digest Books, 1995.

Bender, Sheila, and Christi Killien. *Writing in a New Convertible with the Top Down: A Unique Guide for Writers.* rev. ed. Hilsboro, Ore.: Blue Heron, 1997.

Bennett, Hal Zina. *Write from the Heart: Unleashing the Power of Your Creativity.* 2d rev. ed. Novato, Calif.: New World Library, 2001.

Bernays, Anne, and Pamela Painter. *What If? Writing Exercises for Fiction Writers.* New York: HarperCollins, 1995.

Bradbury, Ray. *Zen in the Art of Writing: Essays on Creativity.* Santa Barbara, Calif.: Joshua Odell Editions, 1994.

Brande, Dorothea. *Becoming a Writer.* Los Angeles: Tarcher, 1934, 1981.

Burroway, Janet. *Writing Fiction: A Guide to Narrative Craft.* 5th ed. New York: Longman, 2000.

Busch, Frederick, ed. *Letters to a Young Fiction Writer.* New York: W.W. Norton, 1999.

Cameron, Julia. *The Artist's Way: A Spiritual Path to Higher Creativity.* New York: Tarcher, 1992.

Collom, Jack, and Sheryl Noethe. *Poetry Everywhere: Teaching Poetry Writing in School and in the Community.* New York: Teachers & Writers Collaborative, 1994.

Daniel, Lois. *How to Write Your Own Life Story.* 3rd ed. Chicago: Chicago Review Press, 1991.

Dillard, Annie. *The Writing Life.* New York: Harper & Row, 1989.

Elbow, Peter. *Writing Without Teachers.* 2nd ed. New York: Oxford University Press, 1998.

Fox, John. *Finding What You Didn't Lose: Expressing Your Truth and Creativity Through Poem-Making.* New York: Putnam, 1995.

———. *Poetic Medicine: The Healing Art of Poem-Making.* New York: Putnam, 1997.

Gardner, John. *The Art of Fiction: Notes on Craft for Young Writers.* New York: Vintage Books, 1991.

Gerard, Philip. *Creative Nonfiction: Researching and Crafting Stories of Real Life.* Cincinnati: Story Press, 1996.

Goldberg, Bonni. *Room to Write: Daily Invitations to a Writer's Life.* New York: Tarcher, 1996.

Goldberg, Natalie. *Writing Down the Bones: Freeing the Writer Within.* Boston: Shambhala, 1986.

———. *Wild Mind: Living the Writer's Life.* New York: Bantam, 1990.

Heffron, Jack. *The Writer's Idea Book*. Cincinnati: Writer's Digest Books, 2000.

Hemley, Robin. *Turning Life into Fiction*. Cincinnati: Story Press, 1994.

Kelton, Nancy Davidoff. *Writing from Personal Experience: How to Turn Your Life into Salable Prose*. Cincinnati: Writer's Digest Books, 1997.

King, Stephen. *On Writing: A Memoir of the Craft*. New York: Scribner, 2000.

Kowit, Steve. *In the Palm of Your Hand: The Poet's Portable Workshop*. Gardiner, Maine: Tilbury House, 1995.

Lamott, Anne. *Bird by Bird: Some Instructions on Writing and Life*. New York: Pantheon, 1994.

Le Guin, Ursula K. *Steering the Craft: Exercises and Discussions on Story Writing for the Lone Navigator or the Mutinous Crew*, Portland, Ore.: The Eighth Mountain Press, 1998.

Lerner, Betsy. *The Forest for the Trees: An Editor's Advice to Writers*. New York: Riverhead Books, 2000.

Maisel, Eric. *Deep Writing: 7 Principles That Bring Ideas to Life*. New York: Tarcher, 1999.

Matson, Clive. *Let the Crazy Child Write: Finding Your Creative Writing Voice*. Novato, Calif.: New World Library, 1998.

Newman, Lesléa. *Writing from the Heart: Inspiration and Exercises for Women Who Want to Write*. Freedom, Calif.: The Crossing Press, 1993.

Perry, Susan K. *Writing in Flow: Keys to Enhanced Creativity*. Cincinnati: Writer's Digest Books, 1999.

Phillips, Jan. *Marry Your Muse: Making a Lasting Commitment to Your Creativity*. Wheaton, Ill.: Quest Books, 1997.

Provost, Gary. *Make Your Words Work: Proven Techniques for Effective*

Writing — for Fiction and Nonfiction. Cincinnati: Writer's Digest Books, 1990.

Ray, Robert. *The Weekend Novelist*. New York: Dell, 1994.

Reeves, Judy. *A Writer's Book of Days: A Spirited Companion & Lively Muse for the Writing Life*. Novato, Calif.: New World Library, 1999.

Rekulak, Jason. *The Writer's Block: 786 Ideas to Jump-Start Your Imagination*. Philadelphia: Running Press, 2001.

Safire, William, and Leonard Safire, eds. *Good Advice on Writing*. New York: Simon & Schuster, 1992.

Shaughnessy, Susan. *Walking on Alligators: A Book of Meditations for Writers*. San Francisco: HarperSanFrancisco, 1993.

Sher, Gail. *One Continuous Mistake: Four Noble Truths for Writers*. New York: Penguin/Arkana, 1999.

———. *The Intuitive Writer: Listening to Your Own Voice*. New York: Penguin/Compass, 2002.

Snow, Kimberley. *Writing Yourself Home: A Woman's Guided Journey of Self Discovery*. Berkeley, Calif.: Conari Press, 1989.

Strunk, William, Jr., and E. B. White. *The Elements of Style*. 4th ed. New York: Allyn and Bacon, 2000.

Thomas, Frank P. *How to Write the Story of Your Life*. Cincinnati: Writer's Digest Books, 1984.

Ueland, Brenda. *If You Want to Write: A Book About Art, Independence, and Spirit*. 2nd ed. St. Paul, Minn.: Graywolf Press, 1987.

Wooldridge, Susan G. *Poemcrazy: Freeing Your Life with Words*. New York: Clarkson Potter, 1996.

Ziegler, Alan. *The Writing Workshop*, Vol. I, New York: Teachers & Writers Collaborative, 1981.

———. *The Writing Workshop*, Vol. II, New York: Teachers & Writers Collaborative, 1984.

ABOUT THE AUTHOR

Judy Reeves teaches writing and leads creative writing workshops at the University of California, San Diego, and California State University, Fullerton, and at The Writers' Room in San Diego. She also teaches at various writers' conferences and seminars. As a member of the Second Story Writers, a women's writing ensemble, two of her plays have been produced. In 1993, she co-founded The Writing Center, a nonprofit literary arts organization. She lives in San Diego where she is at work on a novel. Her Web site is www.JudyReevesWriter.com.

15604713R00117

Made in the USA
Middletown, DE
14 November 2014